About Pfeiffer

Pfeiffer serves the professional development and hands-on resource needs of training and human resource practitioners and gives them products to do their jobs better. We deliver proven ideas and solutions from experts in HR development and HR management, and we offer effective and customizable tools to improve workplace performance. From novice to seasoned professional, Pfeiffer is the source you can trust to make yourself and your organization more successful.

Essential Knowledge Pfeiffer produces insightful, practical, and comprehensive materials on topics that matter the most to training and HR professionals. Our Essential Knowledge resources translate the expertise of seasoned professionals into practical, how-to guidance on critical workplace issues and problems. These resources are supported by case studies, worksheets, and job aids and are frequently supplemented with CD-ROMs, websites, and other means of making the content easier to read, understand, and use.

Essential Tools Pfeiffer's Essential Tools resources save time and expense by offering proven, ready-to-use materials—including exercises, activities, games, instruments, and assessments—for use during a training or team-learning event. These resources are frequently offered in loose-leaf or CD-ROM format to facilitate copying and customization of the material.

Pfeiffer also recognizes the remarkable power of new technologies in expanding the reach and effectiveness of training. While e-hype has often created whizbang solutions in search of a problem, we are dedicated to bringing convenience and enhancements to proven training solutions. All our e-tools comply with rigorous functionality standards. The most appropriate technology wrapped around essential content yields the perfect solution for today's on-the-go trainers and human resource professionals.

Essential resources for training and HR professionals

www.pfeiffer.com

ZERO DEFECT HIRING

A QUICK GUIDE TO **THE MOST IMPORTANT DECISIONS MANAGERS** HAVE TO MAKE

WALTER ANTHONY DINTEMAN

Pfeiffer

A Wiley Imprint

www.pfeiffer.com

Published by Pfeiffer

An Imprint of John Wiley & Sons, Inc.

989 Market Street, San Francisco, CA 94103-1741   www.pfeiffer.com

Pfeiffer books and products are available through most bookstores. To contact Pfeiffer directly call our Customer Care Department within the U.S. at (800) 274-4434, outside the U.S. at (317) 572-3985 or fax (317) 572-4002.

Pfeiffer also publishes its books in a variety of electronic formats. Some content that appears in print may not be available in electronic books.

Printed in the United States of America

ISBN: 0-7879-6496-4

Library of Congress Cataloging-in-Publication Data

Dinteman, Walter Anthony, 1945–

  Zero defect hiring : a quick guide to the most important decisions
managers have to make / by Walter Anthony Dinteman ; foreword by Alan
Schonberg.

      p.   cm.

Includes bibliographical references and index.

  ISBN 0-7879-6496-4 (alk. paper)

  1. Employee selection.   2. Employees—Recruiting.   3. Employment
interviewing.   I. Title.

  HF5549.5.S38 D56   2003

  658.3'11—dc21

                                                      2002154224

Acquiring Editor: Matthew Davis

Director of Development: Kathleen Dolan Davies

Developmental Editor: Susan Rachmeler

Editor: Rebecca Taff

Production Editor: Nina Kreiden

Manufacturing Supervisor: Bill Matherly

Interior Design: Bruce Lundquist

Cover Design: redletterdesign.biz

Printing   10 9 8 7 6 5 4 3 2 1

CONTENTS

FOREWORD

ZERO DEFECT HIRING is an essential read for any manager. In this brief book are all the steps and practices that should be followed in making the right considerations along the road toward a placement decision. Any organization is, ultimately, only as strong as the people who work there. Finding and hiring those people is one of management's most important challenges. This book contains a great deal of collected wisdom distilled into a book that is not only an enjoyable read, but concise enough to fit into the schedules of today's busiest managers. If all managers read and followed the concepts in this book, the vast majority of problems associated with hiring would be eliminated. The result would be a much stronger and more profitable organization. Those of us who make our livelihood serving companies in the search and placement of permanent staff see that a clientele informed in these practices will be much more successful.

Zero Defect Hiring is a winner's guide. The winners are the candidates who emerge from this selection process, the hiring managers who select them, and the organizations that win with the best people working for them.

Alan Schonberg
Chairman Emeritus
Management Recruiters International

PREFACE

OF ALL THE DECISIONS made as a manager, none is more important than the selection of staff. Filling the shoes of a great employee who was promoted can be a daunting task for the most experienced manager. Ironically, training on the hiring process is not given the attention it deserves when managers themselves are selected and given the authority to hire others. In a small business, there may be no HR department to advise or train in the best practices to follow in hiring staff. When a new business is launched, the technical, legal, logistical, and financial issues are so overwhelmingly important that the seemingly mundane task of recruiting and hiring staff is relegated to a lower priority. This, of course, can spell doom for a start-up because nearly every position and hire is crucial to the success of the fledgling enterprise. It takes only one bad mate to sink a ship. In the same way, the success of any size organization ultimately depends on the performance of its employees. Companies that spend a great deal of time on training, development, and evaluation of employees rarely devote as much time or effort to hiring employees in the first place. This book addresses the particular management training issues concerned with the quality of the hiring process.

Much has been written about *total quality management*, but TQM is usually applied to organizations, production, and team management *after* people are hired and in place. So from the very beginning, an organization's effort to raise standards, improve quality, and avoid defects in products and services may be off to a rocky start because the staffing decisions that launched the whole effort were, in themselves, defective.

This concise book is intended as a quick read on the essential aspects of the hiring process. It is universally useful to any hiring managers faced with the challenge of making the right decisions for the best hires for their enterprise no matter their industry and regardless of the size of the organization. Most of the examples in the book pertain to challenges within a corporate, mid-management environment, but most can be easily applied in any setting, including not-for-profit or public sector organizations.

Zero Defect Hiring is about doing the right thing in the hiring process. It is about avoiding common mistakes that both experienced and inexperienced managers often make. Human resource professionals should find it great for review of the practices they knew but may have forgotten. It is about "gut" checks as well as logical procedures that will greatly reduce, if not completely eliminate, problems within the process. The result will be stronger hires and a stronger organization.

Zero Defect Hiring is the compilation of decades of collective wisdom of sales, service, marketing, product, manufacturing, and human resource managers who have learned what works best in the hiring of great employees. These friends and colleagues have much to share also from mistakes for which they paid dearly. These episodes are often humorous, in hindsight, and can be seen as especially so since, if you avoid similar pitfalls, you will never personally have to pay the consequences.

The material in this short book stands alone as both a guide and reference work, but is also the core of a training package. That package includes a *Facilitator's Guide* that leads a management trainer through all of the topics in the form of overviews, discussion questions, and activities. It includes a CD-ROM with all appropriate handouts and PowerPoint® slides covering all main points of the book. A seminar where peers and colleagues interact and participate actively in the learning experience is the recommended way to learn the material and to best ensure a zero defect hiring process.

March 2003

Walter Anthony Dinteman

ACKNOWLEDGMENTS

ZERO DEFECT HIRING would never have come to be had it not been for the many friends and colleagues who encouraged me and who made suggestions for improvement. I wish to thank Tom Taylor, VP of Marketing and Sales at Course Technology, for contributing several key ideas. Jay Heiny, director of recruiting at Prentice-Hall, shared his passion for structured, behavior-based interviewing and encouraged the project at an early stage. Alan Schonberg, founder of Management Recruiters International, has been a constant inspiration. Hy Mariampolski, managing director of Qualidata Research, has shown the humor and fortitude necessary to bring a useful business book to print. The Pfeiffer team of Matthew Davis, Kathleen Dolan Davies, and

Susan Rachmeler has been thoroughly professional in all aspects of sponsorship and development. Susan, in particular, has made many substantive improvements in both content and style. Lastly, *Zero Defect Hiring* and I owe a great deal to my assistant James Arnold Brown, Jr., for his diligence in formatting the book and *Facilitator's Guide* and in editing and preparing the PowerPoint® slides.

Chapter 1

Before You Start Hiring,
Have a Plan

TO BEGIN A ZERO DEFECT HIRING PROCESS, you must have a plan for that task. The old saying "Failing to plan is planning to fail" applies to the important accountability of hiring as well as it does to any other management activity. Here are the most important steps in the planning process:

1. Read and revise, if necessary, the job description for the open position.

2. Make a list with interview questions that pertain to the job description. Include questions from resumes in a folder, along with the resume and application form.

3. Create an objective statement of the clear business need for the position. If the position is a newly created one, this statement is part of the job description and the budget requisition or approval process.

4. Set the salary range budget for the position.

5. Clear any approvals necessary, making certain that the position itself is approved by higher management and the HR department and that the position is included in the budget.

6. Set a target date for the new hire to start within a short, but flexible range.

7. Calendar key events that will lead to the hire.

8. Clear interview times on your calendar.

9. If other people are involved in the process, calendar their available time to participate in the interviews.

Let's examine each of these steps in a little more detail.

The *job description* should be revised periodically to take into account new or added accountabilities such as those that have technological impact. Lately, for example, field sales managers are accountable for training new hires on databases or "customer contact" software. This one difference may mean a new set of skills is needed by the managers being hired as well as by field reps. The advent of team structure on production lines may call for a very different type of employee than in the days before team structures were in place.

All *special attributes or qualities* you are looking for should be incorporated in the hiring plan under a *questions to ask* list. Copy this for the folder to use in every interview with each candidate. Add specific candidate questions derived from the phone screen (the short, initial interview) and resume. Review these questions following behavioral interviewing guidelines (see Chapter 8).

The salary and total compensation package need to be reviewed, approved, and set before the process begins. It can be extremely frustrating for a hiring authority to discover well into the process that excellent candidates turn down jobs because the *offer range* is unrealistically low or that an assumed budget was different (always lower!) than the hiring manager believed. There are several on-line resources that will allow a hiring authority to research market value for almost any job. The best of these adjust for geographic location. Check out www.salary.com for salary comparisons of various geographic regions.

Many companies have a salary matrix in place. This is usually a grid that shows set salary ranges for all approved positions within the organization appropriately labeled and numbered. While this system sometimes limits flexibility in making offers, the fairness and stability it brings outweigh the limitations. Make sure that the job you are hiring for is *approved for the salary level* on the matrix.

Timing is everything in many aspects of life, and this seems especially true in the confluence of events that lead a person to a new career opportunity. The firm should not only have a *hiring timetable,* but the hiring authority must coordinate all schedules on a calendar to ensure that candidates are available and all interviewers are aware and ready to participate in the process in a timely manner.

It is a good rule to have a best start date in mind, but never feel compelled to hire to a deadline. First, say, you plan to hire within one month. You have done all the pre-hire process planning steps outlined above, but you must remember that hiring a top candidate trumps any specific date on a calendar. If missing the target hire date by a few days, or weeks, means the assurance of a more qualified candidate coming along, by all means wait. We'll review this idea further—balanced with the pitfalls of procrastination—in Chapter 17.

Your Key Event Calendar should block out specific times and days for the hiring process. Here's an itemized list of suggested events and considerations that impact the events calendar:

- *Contact a professional recruiter* (more about this in Chapter 6). A professional recruiter can help in every area covered by this book—if he or she can't (or won't), don't work with that recruiter!

- *Place ads on the Internet and/or in newspapers or journals,* taking into account the new job description. (Ads are covered in Chapter 4.) Budget for both time and money in this investment. Planning can save a lot of money in this department.

- *Designate resume and application reviewing time.* Managers often fail to realize they really do need quality time to review applications, cover letters, and resumes. Putting this activity off usually means short-changing this part of the process. Zero defect hiring means attending to such details with time blocked out for this purpose alone.

- *Phone screen "paper qualified applicants,"* that is, those meeting the minimum standards set. Again, you need to plan for these short (fifteen to thirty minute) information exchanges. In larger firms, the HR department may handle this level of interviewing. In many cases, however, managers prefer to handle even telephone screening.

- *Set times for first round interviews.* Whether you are bringing someone in or going to see that person, planning is crucial, especially as to the exact timing of the interview. If you are seeing more than one candidate, allow thirty minutes between interviews to refresh, take notes, and review information for the next interview.

- *Set times for second level interviews.* This may be even more crucial to plan ahead, as "second level" usually means more people involved and perhaps a visit by the candidate to the home office for an entire day of multiple interviews.

- *Make all travel arrangements as far ahead as possible* whether the manager or the candidate must travel for the interview. Calendar the latest date for an economical trip to be arranged. Despite the fact that most managers are well aware of the cost penalties on airfare alone in last minute arrangements, costly delays in planning happen often. One manager was embarrassed to have to turn in a $3,500 charge on his expense account due to missing a window of travel opportunity. Had he planned the travel day in advance, he would have saved at least $2,500.

- Count backwards to the present from the target start date to *allow for a candidate's customary two-week notice* (or more for some high-level positions) and for other days within the hiring process time.

- *Make sure anyone involved in the final decision is available on specified dates.* It can be embarrassing as well as bad for one's career to leave key people out of the hiring process. At the same time, you don't want the organization to look overly bureaucratic by continuing to delay the second level interview "until we can round everybody up." Good planning will make for a seamless process internally.

- *Avoid holiday travel periods* in the process, or plan to work around them. Don't subject yourself or your candidate to these horrors. Block out dates immediately before and after holidays as unavailable for travel.

- Beyond the mechanics and logistics, *make sure you have buy-in on the attributes and basic qualifications of the candidates to be interviewed.* The date that discussion will be held should also be on the planning calendar, especially in the context of a large organization.

In summary, the initial planning for hiring is a crucial part of the process. Mistakes in selection criteria, bad timing, backtracking for approvals, and a host of other problems can be avoided simply by laying out all the steps in the process that you can before you start. This way you start on the right foot toward zero defect hiring.

Chapter 2

Paint a Picture
of the Perfect Hire

WELL, BECAUSE NOBODY'S PERFECT, we won't attempt to re-create any saints here! But it doesn't hurt to use your imagination to paint a picture of an ideal candidate—the number of years of experience, past accomplishments, and key attributes that generally spell success in the position. Everyone has some defects or shortcomings. This book is not about weeding out defective people. As all people are imperfect, you'd never be able to hire anyone if that were the case. This book is about *avoiding defects in the process* of hiring the best-fit people you can find. To help visualize a realistic portrait, here are some things to keep in mind:

- *Beware of the tendency to mirror,* that is, to be positively inclined toward people who seem to be just like you. One candidate may seem very strong due to physical attributes like yours—it is human nature to give a

slight, even unconscious, edge to people like our-
selves. This is not to say that this person wouldn't be
an excellent hire. Just be aware that you may be insuf-
ficiently critical and overlook issues simply because
you instantly liked the candidate. Mirroring is to be
avoided because you tend to overlook potential problem areas in a candidate's background due to his or
her seemingly overarching likeness to yourself—and
we all know how successful you are! Now this doesn't
mean to avoid hiring your clone. But you just might
consider a deeper evaluation of all credentials, references, and so forth than usual, simply because they
look so superficially perfect.

- *Be wary also of the halo effect,* that is, people to whom you
  respond favorably because they remind you of some
  successful person you know. This form of prejudice is
  related to mirroring—we could call it a "portrait"
  effect. Here you need to check out real attributes and
  performance compared to the picture someone pre-
  sents, again due to superficial qualities that look familiar. Hiring a person who seems to wear the same halo
  as another successful person may make you less
  inclined to see that person as the individual he or she
  is. Just because someone is a "dead ringer" or "acts
  like" another successful person or was in that person's
  fraternity or sorority does not make him or her ideal
  for the position.

- *List background behavioral attributes of your model candidate* to look for in the real people you interview. This
  means using the logic that a person who measures up to

certain levels of *talent, experience, and skill,* as demonstrated through real life experiences required for the position, could be an excellent potential employee. What should the successful candidate have done? What traits predict success in the position? Does success in college seem to predict job success as demonstrated by most other people who hold this position? What about high energy as shown by capacity for long hours, participation in demanding sports activities, or some other context where energy is a common denominator of success? Sticking to this list will make a profile much stronger and less likely to be skewed by irrelevant (and possibly illegal) factors such as sex and age. (More about this in Chapter 4.)

- *Separate behavioral attributes from trained skills* when describing the ideal candidate. You may indeed want both a "persuasive" individual and one who can close a sale. *Persuasion* is a behavioral attribute and, while *persuasive skills* can be taught, the inclination for that talent is usually there already. Closing techniques, on the other hand, are more specific skills that can be readily taught to someone with persuasive talent. (Interviewing questions to determine these sorts of distinctions are covered in Chapter 7.) Now if skills must be learned for the new job, you would want to concentrate on the candidate's ability to learn, not necessarily on the person's current possession of a skill. You would ask what else he or she had learned and how the person learned it. To be sure, a candidate who would require less training could be an asset in terms of costs, up-and-running time, and so on, but you should determine the relative weight of a person's raw talent against experience and skills already possessed.

- *Think about the diverse people in the organization,* who may be different from one another but share common success rates. Sometimes exceptions not only prove the rule, they *are* the rule. One company's most successful sales rep ever was an older woman in a career change following twenty years as a homemaker. She did not fit the model in work experience of a typical employee in outside sales. Her success opened many doors that had previously been closed to people in her personal situation. Another company took a chance in hiring an immigrant from a Second World country. He, too, became the top-producing rep of that organization, overcoming numerous biases to prove himself and the value of diversity. Almost any organization benefits from the differences various employees bring to the table. Think about differences as well as similarities to successful people and you will be less likely to exclude the next great hire because of prejudice about what a successful person looks like rather than how he or she behaves.

- *Consider a candidate's values and make sure they mesh with the company values and culture.* An article in *Fortune Small Business* says that a lack of alignment on values is a greater cause for lack of success than deficiencies in skills ("Build an 'A' Team," March 2002,

Verne Harnish). In the wake of the Enron/Andersen scandal, many companies have reviewed their ethical guidelines and are making sure that company values are known and practiced by all employees. For most, this means that they must make sure that newcomers understand what the company believes in. It may seem obvious that you would want to hire "honest" employees. This may be so obvious that it would be an assumption and thus overlooked as something to determine in the character of a prospective employee. Consider the definition that values are "the beliefs held that help an individual make right and ethical decisions, even when a specific rule may not exist or be known." An example is this: If an individual knows and believes that offering bribes is wrong, he or she would be unlikely to do so. The person would be reinforced in his or her beliefs by a company value statement that was incorporated into a policy that called for "honest and straightforward dealing with all customers." In describing the ideal hire, it makes sense to remind oneself that it is important to get at "values and ethics" in the selection process. It is possible to uncover even something as intangible as candidates' values by asking questions about decisions they have made. (See Chapter 8 on behavioral interviewing on this point.)

The point of this discussion is that, while a hiring manager should have a good idea of what he or she is looking for, there remains a need to be open-minded about hiring the right person based primarily on fit for the job. Fit is best determined by close examination of a person's past behavior in applicable situations likely to be confronted on the job. The perfect hire may or may not fit the portrait originally envisioned, but the differences will be ones that are seen as positive attributes for the job at hand.

Chapter 3

Write a **Motivating** Ad

FIRST, DETERMINE THE ADVERTISING BUDGET and choose where the ad will be placed. The choice of where to run ads is mostly dependent on the audience for the ad. Certain trade journals are appropriate to their particular industries. Newspapers are generally good for local pools in metropolitan areas and for lower-level positions. The Internet is fast becoming the venue of choice for all employment ads. Some industries, such as information and telecommunications, use the Internet far more than any other resource. The Internet itself has thousands of job boards, some with highly specialized focus.

Budget considerations can be significant. A 4" × 6" executive search ad in *The Wall Street Journal* can cost $18,000. Typical smaller ads in most metropolitan newspapers' Sunday editions (by far the best day to run an ad) run several thousand dollars on average. Even Internet ads, unless the firm has a favorable subscription rate, can cost several hundred dollars. This is one area where working with a recruiting firm can actually save considerable sums, given the mass buying power the larger firms can bring to getting discount rates on print and electronic ads.

Some firms require internal posting of positions for present employees to consider and apply before a position can be posted or advertised externally. Check to make sure no such policy exists or that the internal requirement has been met.

Whether you choose to advertise the open position in a newspaper, in a journal, or on the Internet, you need to make that posting as attractive and motivational as possible. This is the case whether your company is one of the Fortune 500 or a small business.

In periods of higher unemployment, some companies take an arrogant stance in thinking that "people want to work for us because we are the biggest player in the industry, and people will do anything to work here." The truth is that the managerial and professional segment represents a very low unemployment sector within the U.S. labor force. Even in the post–September 11 recession, that segment is under 3.2 percent, according to the U.S. Bureau of Labor Statistics. Perhaps more importantly, most job changes occur among *employed* people, so managers shouldn't assume that they can be less than their competitive best.

Given the limitations of size and budget, great ads should do the following:

- *Call potential applicants to action.* Motivating means getting people to move, so use words that call for action.

Action is what the ad is about, so ask for it! Instead of "the world's leading widget manufacture seeks qualified individuals . . ." say, "Join the #1 widget maker. . . ."

- *Lead with the highest competitive salary range approved for the position*, provided, of course, your company's policy permits this disclosure. Those that do have an attention-getting advantage and it is, after all, a fact that emerges early in the recruiting process. Instead of using "$50,000+" or "$50,000 to $75,000," it's better to hold out the maximum carrot: "up to $75,000 for the right fit individual." If your company is truly competitive or aggressive with salaries, use this advantage to pull underpaid candidates to the job. The best-fit person is worth the high end of the salary range.

- *List key requirements.* Make sure the requirements really are baseline prerequisites, often determined by company policy. List the top three job requirements as short, bulleted items. Remember, the point here is not so much to fully inform applicants as it is to *attract and motivate* them to apply. You will have plenty of opportunities to probe requirements and screen out bad matches on the requirement side.

- *List key accountabilities* without the details of a job description. It is a good idea to briefly list the duties, but not spell them out as in an employment contract. These kinds of details can come out in the interview process. Many ads say way too much in the job description. Succinct bullets work in listing accountabilities, too. Again, the ad is intended to draw responses, not to fully inform the public.

- *Include an Equal Employment Opportunity statement* in all ads. Basically, this states that your company does not discriminate against people based on race, religion, national origin, color, sex, marital status, change in marital status, pregnancy, age, or physical handicap. (See Chapter 10 for more on this topic.)

- *Specifically forbid phone calls.* Not only are these calls a waste of your time, but also by accepting phone calls on initial responses, you have, in effect, granted an interview to a candidate who may be only marginally qualified. Your contact information should be blind. Make up an anonymous box number specific to each posting. This makes it easy to separate mail. In the same way, it is better to use a dedicated e-mail address just for the incoming resumes—there could be thousands!

- *Require a cover letter as well as a resume.* By requiring an original, job-specific cover letter, you can eliminate a lot of pseudo candidates who may just be fishing for a change rather than those truly interested in the position. The cover letter requirement can specify that the applicant "write a paragraph on your understanding of the position and company" (if this was revealed). Experience shows that this one small requirement screens out at least three-quarters of the undesirable candidates from the people you really want to talk to.

Some of the small hurdles in the early stage of the hiring process can be useful indicators of strengths and fit for the opportunity. The ad is the place to start. For example, those who adhere to the application requirements set forth in the ad will, most likely, be the more detail-oriented and conscientious employees. Those who don't? Well, see Chapter 12 on "red flags"!

Chapter 4

Read, but **Don't Rely** on, Resumes

MOST HIRING MANAGERS CONSIDER THE RESUME to be the central document in the hiring process. It should not be. In 1999, an MRI survey of thousands of resumes showed that nearly 92 percent contained false or misleading information. More importantly, you must *remember that you have to hire a person, not a piece of paper.* Some recruiting firms routinely avoid resumes in favor of more comprehensive data sheets, formal application forms, and in-depth screening interviews to more accurately summarize a person's fit for a particular opportunity. A formal application usually has a signature line where a candidate verifies accuracy of all information.

However, since most hiring authorities do work with resumes, consider the following points and hints:

- *Sometimes good people write bad resumes.* Because of a lack of training or experience in writing resumes, a qualified person could put in too much detail or not "market" himself or herself well by positioning or highlighting relevant experience. This is especially the case with a passive candidate who is not presently even looking for a job change. In many cases the best candidate may be working for a direct competitor and not be seeking a change simply because he or she does not know about the opportunity. In this case, motivation in constructing a good, current resume is lacking. The potentially great candidate produces a weak document simply because he or she is not driven to do better or has a bit of arrogance in presenting only bare essentials without any details about accomplishments.

- *Sometimes less-qualified people write great resumes.* The advent of word processing and spelling and grammar checkers has eliminated much illiteracy from resumes. People with little experience can look better by following a good resume-writing book. Remember, the unemployed active candidate may have the most time and creativity to devote to the composition of an excellent-looking resume. This does not mean that unemployed people should be avoided—there are many very legitimate reasons for unemployment, especially in a downsizing environment. It does mean that those who are unemployed should and do often have well-crafted resumes, some directed and critiqued by professional outplacement services.

- *Read between the lines in every resume.* For example, a gap between jobs can be concealed by from-to employment dates rounded off to years rather than months. It is OK for someone to be unemployed for weeks or even months, but the more time between jobs, the more explanation that is required. Many people regard time off between jobs as problematic. It may be. But it is more of a problem if the candidate attempts to hide the gap or lie about it. It is best if the person owns up to the time between jobs. Seeing time off accurately described as, for example, "a sabbatical taken for travel and catching up with family before the next job" is better than having it come out later that the candidate left job one in April and didn't go to job two until November, with absolutely no explanation of the gap. A word of warning here: Avoid probing if the gap had anything to do with any medical condition or pregnancy. The candidate does owe an explanation of gaps in employment but must volunteer the information.

- *Look for puffery such as title inflation.* Banks are notorious for their number of "vice presidents." Every inside-sales telemarketer for one telecomm company was called a "sales engineer." Of course, what people actually did and accomplished is more important than any title. The problem is that one company may actually have a position of sales engineer that sold and installed the product and another using that title for marketing a technical product. One cannot assume that a title implies a job category that translates from one company to another.

- *Look for actions and results versus job descriptions.* Sure, the title and one-line definition may be necessary, but what someone did in his or her last position is more pertinent. "Hired five people and had lowest turnover in the division" is an action/result statement. "Ran five-person section" is not.

- *Accomplishments are an important hiring factor.* If someone were really successful in his or her job, he or she would be more than happy to include the percentage of revenue increase, or the amount of money saved, or the prizes he or she won, or the recognition he or she received. Absence of any accomplishments and the metrics that go with them can be an oversight. If there are not many accomplishments and no supporting data, that's a red flag. While quantification of results is not always easy to cite, those who can and do this are more often the stronger candidates. "Action resulted in a 76 percent increase in customer retention" is that sort of statement. This kind of precise accomplishment statement also gives the hiring manager a specific point to verify in the reference check.

- *Review the cover letter.* The best cover letters should detail what a person knows about the job for which he or she is applying and why he or she would be a good fit. Experience shows that people who are just window shopping for jobs will not go to the trouble to compose an original, job-specific cover letter.

- *Check on the candidate's knowledge of your company.* These days most people seeking employment have access to the Internet at home, school, or the public library. Today's savvy applicant should go to your company's website and be conversant with your company and familiar with its products. References to this research should show up in the cover letter or, if not, then should certainly be mentioned in the first interview.

• *Look for exaggeration, if not outright lies.* Most resumes contain gaps, intentional or otherwise. Areas most often fudged include (a) number of direct reports versus "dotted line" reports to enhance management accountability; (b) GPA (nobody "forgets" a GPA, but when they "cannot recall," it was usually below 3.0); (c) rankings among salespeople—again, high, verifiable rankings are known with increases in results to the correct decimal point, while low ones are "unknown" or "forgotten"; (d) references to accomplishments or awards, without much detail. Ask for proof of all such information.

Many of the above examples are from the world of sales, but the counterparts of these kinds of proofs of accomplishment do exist in operations, finance, research, and production. For example, financial managers, when successful, save money and meet reporting deadlines. They are recognized for their achievements, and both qualitative and quantitative examples can be cited. Accomplished employees in operations management also meet deadlines, save money, and have low employee turnover rates. Again, these are all *results* that simply mean more than the statement of job accountability.

Beyond the resume is the structured interview. To prepare for the interview, use various resume facts as a starting point:

- *Use behavioral interviewing based in some part on the resume.* Ask for the full explanation and story behind all key experience listed in the resume. If an executive candidate "participated in the IPO," make a note in your "questions to ask" file to get at exactly what that role was and, specifically, what actions were personally taken in that capacity.

- *Check all major resume claims in the reference checking process.* Ask the candidate's permission to verify the information via a thorough reference check. You might be surprised by backpedaling in the interview. Say, "Can you provide a copy of your certification document in network programming?" If the person offers an excuse or resistance to such requests, he or she probably does not want you to check.

While the resume is considered a basic must-have document, one should never rely on it to make anything but minimal decisions on where to start and who to include in the initial pool of candidates. The resume should be the basis of further questions. Be skeptical and don't take statements that appear on a resume as proof of qualifications. (See Appendix A for examples of both a poorly written and a better resume.)

Chapter 5

Always **Create a Pool**
of Candidates

HAVING CHOICES IS BETTER than not having them. If we can make that assumption, it follows that creating a pool of candidates from which to choose is a good idea. The minimal definition of a "pool" is two or more applicants for the position, but in the largest sense it also means the list of all potential candidates, including rejected ones. Here are some thoughts on the subject of the candidate pool:

- Even if you already have a strong candidate for a given position, it makes good sense to *challenge that person* by seeing how other potential competitors for the position match up. If nothing else, you will validate the choice you wanted to make in the first place.

- At this point the internal candidate must be considered. This may involve company politics as well as policy. Most companies give first consideration to current employees who apply for a promotion. While there are many benefits to an organization in promoting from within, the truly objective candidate search would *put the internal candidate into the pool for examination against outside contenders.* Many companies will simply evaluate an internal candidate and decide to promote or pass over the employee before opening the search to the outside. It is a very good idea to determine what the policy is on this matter before proceeding with an outside search.

- *People who pass the telephone screening step are in the true pool of candidates.* Telephone screens are usually short, basic information calls that establish the candidate's fundamental understanding of the job and your clarification of any qualifying points in the resume.

- After screening candidates by phone or in person, *you will ideally have anywhere from five to ten people to see face-to-face* for an in-depth interview. The first face-to-face interview should continue the information exchange and should also go into the behavioral attributes, as discussed in Chapter 8. In larger firms, the HR department may handle the process to this point before handing off selection interviewing to the hiring manager.

- *Your plan should provide for taking three to five people to the second level,* where the interviews continue the behavioral questions. At this point you not only have a second interview, but you also would involve a peer, your boss, or a potential peer of the candidates. At this level, you are attempting to reduce your choice to the two best, if not verifying that you have a clear winner you want to hire.

- This is the point where *you must check references.* Some firms and many recruiters do not consider the pool to be valid unless references have been checked for individuals who are in it. This is not a bad idea, but is often not followed for practical, time, and resource reasons. That said, there is no good reason for not checking references when the candidate pool is down to final contenders.

- *The finalist(s) should be taken through the firm to meet and be interviewed by more personnel,* including HR, where benefits can be discussed. Increasingly, benefits are a crucial factor in a person's decision to accept a job offer. Candidates have been known to leave the pool if the package looks unacceptable. More often, HR can offer a benefits picture that helps close a hire or continues to make the finalists enthusiastic members of the pool.

- Finally, and this is a somewhat controversial point, *avoid hiring your second-choice* candidate. Someone (you?) saw something in the second-choice person that, compared to Number One, was regarded as a defect. It is very tempting to simply hire the back-up person. If Number One fails to accept an offer or if some other interviewer thinks your Number One is Number Two, pause and reflect on this disagreement.

Make sure there are no misunderstandings of fact. Given reasonable time, try to create a new pool that includes the second-choice person. In other words, challenge that candidate with other choices and other avenues of interviewing (other players, new probes, new tests). If the former Number Two is then regarded as a top choice, he or she is no longer a runner-up.

The idea of creating a pool is all about choice. Having a strong pool of candidates is just one more way to ensure fewer defects in the hiring process.

Chapter 6

Use Recruiters to **Raise the Quality** of the Hiring Process

ALL THINGS CONSIDERED, using professional recruiting services is smart business. Very often, however, recruiters are not used due to the assumption that their services are expensive and not essential to the process. Why should you use recruiters?

First, *professional recruiting is a dedicated service*, whereas that activity within a company is a sideline, well down the list of duties of a typical manager's job description. Even when an HR department employs full-time recruiters, they usually have far fewer resources to apply to the process than even an average-sized recruiting office. Even a small recruiting firm can, for example, make thousands of calls to uncover passive candidates rather than searching job boards for active job seekers floating resumes on the Internet. Particularly in that endeavor, a recruiting firm has the time, manpower, and expertise to sort, qualify, and initially screen thousands of resumes. Individuals working part-time cannot do this process efficiently and in a timely fashion.

A second reason for using these services is that *there are many savings to be gained* in the use of professional recruiters—both in search costs, such as discounted advertising, and in an indirect way, such as opportunity costs. Very often companies bury or ignore the opportunity costs they pay due to extended periods of having key positions open: loss of revenue, loss of the interviewer's time, and the loss of other employees' time or productivity because they are doing the work of the open position in addition to the job they are paid to do. One way to measure the opportunity cost of an open sales position, for example, is to look at the top line of revenue that position is expected to produce, then divide that number by the typical two hundred working days in a year. With this formula, the costs of an open territory with a $2,000,000 base are $10,000 per day. By reducing the length of a search in the case just cited, a professional recruiter might save the company $10,000 *per day.*

Before discussing the value of professional recruiting services further, let's look at the two major kinds of recruiting firms and the ways in which they differ. One type is the *retained* search firm. These recruiters are typically paid an initial fee to conduct searches for any open positions a company may have, with a certain balance paid on placement. In some cases, an annual retainer is paid in addition to specific placement fees. The other type of recruiting firm is called *contingency* because fees are paid only when a placement is actually made, that is, usually no up-front fees are paid to contingency recruiters.

Sometimes a hybrid of the two involves an *engagement* fee of one third of the total expected fee.

Regardless of the type of firm or payment structure, *the average fees for recruiting are between 20 and 30 percent of the hire's first-year compensation.* Compensation can include a projected bonus, but is often defined as salary alone. Thus, an accepted $50,000 salary offer would mean a fee of $10,000 to $15,000 to the recruiter. As with any major consumer decision, it pays to do some background checks and cost comparisons among recruiting firms. It is certainly safe to choose a nationally known company, but some independents are also good and may charge lower fees. In any case, it is best to know the individual recruiter and his or her specialty. The more closely related the recruiter's experience is to the client company's product and services, the more likely the recruiter will succeed. This is obviously a more important consideration than saving a relatively small amount of money in fees.

Here's a quick list of value-added services that a professional recruiter brings to the hiring process, making high-sounding fees justifiable:

- *Advertising can be paid for or greatly discounted by recruiters.* A well-connected firm can obtain 75 percent or greater reductions on national classified ads, which can be negotiated as "extras" or included in the fee.

- *Recruiters are in daily contact with passive candidates,* who are often among the best choices for a given job. These people may currently hold the exact position at a competitor. Very often, client companies are reluctant to raid their competitors for talent but are happy to use recruiters to entice people away.

- *Professional recruiters screen all candidates,* thus weeding out inappropriate candidates and allowing the company to begin interviewing on a higher level.

- *Better recruiters do deeper qualification of candidates* than employers on such matters as willingness to relocate and job change buy-in on the part of the whole family, not just the candidate.

- *Full-service recruiters provide testing services to clients.* Brainbench™ assessment services, for example, are used to test a variety of computer-related competencies. This service is usually provided at nominal or no extra charge to clients.

- *Good recruiters do complete and thorough reference checking.* (See Appendix B for a sample reference check form.) Additionally, if it is appropriate to the position and called for by company policy, financial credit reports and drug screens can also be obtained.

- *The recruiter acts as a counselor to a candidate and consultant to a client company.* Typically, the recruiter is in a very good position to negotiate salary on behalf of the company. He or she can determine the minimum acceptable salary level and put this in the overall context of the opportunity (for example, career advancement). This may carry more weight than the same discussion conducted by a company employee.

- *Full-service recruiters also handle the logistics of relocation* and can save employers and employees thousands of dollars due to leveraging rock-bottom "preferred vendor" rates on real estate services, van lines, and other major costs of moving.

- *Coordination of the whole process* can be a logistical nightmare for a hiring authority, but is routine for a professional recruiter. Interview times, plane tickets, family house-hunting trips, and so forth can all be done with "one-call shopping" to the recruiter. And, once again, this should be at no extra charge.

For all of the above reasons, it is no wonder the professional recruiting business thrives in the competitive world economy today. As mentioned earlier, fees of 20 to 30 percent of first-year compensation are typical. Some firms might be resistant to paying $90,000 to hire a $300,000 executive. However, such an executive would likely be someone with the skills and experience to manage many people and tens of millions of dollars in revenue. In that context, $90,000 for the right person is a small investment for the return expected and accountabilities assumed. Not finding the right person can obviously cost a whole lot more than the fee paid to a recruiter for the right person.

Chapter 7

Differentiate Talent and Ability
from **Skill and Experience**

IT IS COMMON WISDOM that what people have actually done is more important than what they say they will do. Rather than just imagining what people would do, it is much better to look closely at their actions, behavior, and results from the past. Related to learning about past behavior is understanding differences between talent and ability on one hand and skills and experience on the other. You should not only look for a specific skill or experience closely matched to the tasks that will be required in the new job, but the talent and ability to learn, adapt, and acquire new skills. Here are some points to consider that will help to determine a right fit beyond the scope of specific skills and experience:

- *A hiring manager must evaluate related rather than specifically matched skills.* A good line of questioning is: "Can you tell me about a time that you had to balance and prioritize among several tasks at the same time? What were the circumstances and how did you handle them?" It does not matter that the person's experience was in a completely different environment if what you are trying to determine is that person's capacity for multitasking. What matters is his or her ability and talent for doing that in any situation.

- It is especially true of entry-level positions that a hiring manager identifies talent and ability. What he or she really wants to find out is *how likely the candidate is to be willing and able to accept training* and become the knowledgeable person needed. "Tell me about how you learned the technical specifications of Ztech software. How long did it take you to get up and running?" Not too long ago, companies in the information technology industry would hire just about anyone with the barest minimum skill set needed. COBOL programmers were given high-paying jobs regardless of any other attributes they may or may not have had. No probing of such qualities as *reliability* or *dependability* were considered in the name of expediency to hire people who might rescue the company from the pending Y2K crisis. Now managers charged with hiring programmers are better served by finding out not only whether a programmer can create programs, but also whether or not he or she will show up for work on time or work overtime if needed to complete a project.

- Prior knowledge of a product line would be handy for a candidate to have if he or she were going to sell or market it. If the manager decides that a certain level of knowledge is crucial, then he or she should test for that knowledge. However, *virtually any skill that a person can be trained on should not be a requirement of a job.* Sure, some technical jobs (computer programming, for example) may have a huge pool of highly trained individuals who possess the specific skill level required for consideration. Those candidates would have the baseline or prerequisite skill, but that does not *differentiate* candidates who have this skill for the purpose of selection. Talent and ability to learn other programming languages, or adapt other skills, or, simply, to demonstrate better programming talent than another candidate is much more important than the skill itself.

- Another consideration is this: *"What does this person bring to the position that someone could not be trained on?"* For example, no one can train a person to be energetic. If the job requires high levels of energy, ask about that in this way: "Jill, can you tell me about a long day you worked recently? When did you start? Were there several days like that on your job? What kinds of recreation are you into?" Long days and diverse physical activity do tend to predict high energy levels. Again, look at actual behavior, not imagined behavior. "What do you like to do?" is a lot weaker than "What do you do to energize yourself?"

- Much as you wish you could, *you can't make someone smart.* Again, you have to rely on evidence. If past experience shows you that only highly intelligent people succeed in the position you are hiring for, then you should determine intelligence—or even test for it. Be sure that any test given is standard for all applicants in a pool. Grade point average (GPA) is a shortcut in determining quality of learning, but not all smart people did well in school. If someone didn't do so well academically, you may find other examples of intelligence or creativity. "Can you tell me about a complex problem you had to resolve at the Ztech Company?" You should be more interested in this sort of creative intelligence than academic proof, although getting at both is a good practice.

Another point about school performance: a C average may not be good enough for one company, but an average of mostly A's in a major with an occasional D or F that averages out to a C is probably better than solid C's and D's. Some companies want to see a transcript or a statement about GPA. A hiring manager cannot obtain a transcript, but can require the candidate to produce one for an application process.

- *Work performance is more important than school performance the longer a person has been out of school.* It matters little what GPA a candidate had ten years ago if his or her work performance record has been solid since graduation. But for recent college grads, school is the equivalent of work, and checking academic performance as you would check job references is a good idea.

Understand the differences between attributes that can be learned versus those that are more deeply ingrained in character, or at least learned at an early age. In formulating interview questions, a hiring manager should develop probing questions that reveal underlying talent and ability rather than more superficial attributes, such as those exhibited by narrow experience or specific skills.

Chapter **8**

Interview on **Behavior and Experiences**, Not on Hypotheses

THE BEST PREDICTOR OF FUTURE SUCCESS is past performance. That statement is one version of the wisest observation a hiring authority can make. Another is this: *It is a lot more important to consider what someone has done rather than what he says he will do.* There are many other ways of stating this truth. Almost any experienced manager agrees with these statements, and yet *hypothetical* lines of questioning in interviewing persist. One interview method, *behavioral interviews*, examines the traits and attributes of an individual based on real actions in real situations in which that person has found himself or herself. In contrast, hypothetical interviewing uses the imagination of events, artificial scenarios, and contrived situations. Perhaps because they can be so "imaginative" and "creative," hypothetical questions survive despite all efforts to train managers to the contrary.

A hiring manager once asked this writer, "What would you do if someone gave you an elephant?" This is what we'll call a "Miss America scenario." What did the manager intend by asking such a question? Was he testing a curve ball, looking for a sense of humor, or did he have a collection of favorite answers he could use as matches to screen out undesirable employees? The truth is he really had no good reason. Fortunately, he liked my response: "Gosh, George, what does that have to do with my ability to sell your product?" Since it really had nothing to do with it, we moved on to more relevant subjects, such as sales records.

Here are some examples of behavioral questions that get at real experiences:

- "Can you tell me about a time when you won a major account? Describe an actual situation and what you did to win. It matters little whether this was a big deal or a small, everyday event."

Some candidates will say something like, "I always try to get the client talking so I can determine needs." Well, that's good, but it is much more valuable information if the person describes a specific case: "I asked how his engineering department handled the distribution of data from the branch offices, uncovered the need for a more systematic approach to data collection, and was able to lead him to the Ztech product. They bought a $55,000 package." In the earlier example, the candidate describes theory; in the latter, he shows specific practice.

- "I see here in your cover letter that you are a 'high energy person.' Tell me about the longest day you worked in the past month. When did you start and finish? What did you accomplish? How did you feel the next day?"

One candidate said, "I worked all day and didn't get home until 8:00 p.m." The hiring manager had not seen the underside of a day that short in quite a while. If that candidate considered that an unusually long day, what does that say about energy? Another applicant in the same pool had worked as an election aide for a winning candidate for the state senate. "Well, the most I have worked in one day was actually over three days—36 hours without sleep."

- "We have all lost a few big deals. Can you tell be about one in which you gave it your best but did not succeed? What did you learn from that experience?"

With this sort of setup and probing, the candidate is more likely to own up to some negative experience, which is usually difficult to learn from a candidate primed to always tell about only positive experiences. The interviewer should be interested in whether or not the candidate learned from a mistake.

- "In this new job, you'll be managing several individuals. Can you describe the most difficult individual you ever managed and how you coped?" Again, here is a chance to get at some potentially negative experiences. *How it was handled* is the important aspect of the answer, more so than the outcome. However, the answer might also reveal an issue. Suppose the candidate did not perform well in the situation described, blamed the situation on others or the company, and did not learn from the experience. This could be a red flag.

- "Were you ever asked to do anything that you regarded as unethical? What was the situation, and how did you handle it?"

This kind of question speaks to ethics and values and is an example or probing for experience in intangible areas. Think how much weaker it would be to ask the hypothetical question, "What would you do if someone offered you a kickback or bribe?" Everyone flatly refuses, right?

It takes a lot of thought to come up with questions that get to the heart of the talent, ability, skills, and experience you want a new hire to bring to the job. Take time to think about the big picture, that is, the whole job description, and then break down the components.

Which of these elements would you feel most comfortable training an individual to perform? Toss out most of these from the interview plan. That's because you want to hire someone who brings certain attributes to the table, not just skills you may train her on after she starts. Let's revisit the topic of questions in this light.

If you had said, "What do you do to win business?" you might get a lot of platitudes about how to sell something, but all that really matters is what actions were actually taken in a real situation. Instead of "I build rapport with all my customers," by asking for a real example you might hear this: "I found out from a secretary that the CEO was a die-hard Red Sox fan, so I used some entertainment money to get him play-off tickets." The first hypothetical answer could easily be given by anyone. No progress toward a decision can be made with questions or answers like that one. The real experience answer, on the other hand, regardless of what you may think about it, has substance, which incrementally helps the hiring manager make a decision.

Since you cannot train a person to have energy, or be smart, or use good judgment, these are traits that you may want to uncover through behavioral questions.

- For energy, ask about hard work done, physical activity, and recreation; for intelligence ask about books, interests, hobbies, and grades; for judgment go for an explanation of how big decisions in the past were made (buying a house or a car; looking for a job; selecting a major in college).

- Most people are reluctant to reveal any failure in an interview for a job. Disarm this reluctance by prefacing the question with a negative experience of your own. "Mary, we have all had setbacks. I think I have learned as much from a loss as I have from a win. Tell me about a situation where you gave it your best shot but didn't prevail. What is your assessment of what went wrong?"

- If a key skill is, say, managing ten people, it is useful to know about that skill and experience. Some positive versions of the same sort of question would be, "Which employee did you have the most success in growing and training? What were his or her results? Any awards? Why do you think you were successful with that individual?" If you must ask a theoretical question such as "Mary, what do you think motivates people?" by all means follow up with questions that probe for examples of motivating techniques or rewards showing up in the candidate's personal experience or in those factors the person observed among colleagues or with direct reports. That takes the hypothetical into the real world.

- If you stick to the behavioral and experiential path of questioning, you can uncover the good, the bad, and the ugly in someone's past. People who are proud of their behavior usually have a tale of some test of character they can point to. A good line of questions is, "What was the most difficult obstacle you had to overcome to get where you are today? What were the steps you took? Why did it take so long?"

- You can get at qualities as intangible as one's values if you ask well-conceived and structured behavioral questions that include past value judgments. For example, if you wanted to learn about work ethic or the capacity for dedicated hard work and balancing that with personal life ask, "Jack, we all struggle with trying to balance work with our personal lives. Tell me, how do you do that on a weekly basis?" The answer to that question would be a lot better than the answer to, "How would you handle an assignment that required a lot of overtime, and what effect would that have on your personal life?" The former is grounded in reality, the latter in fantasy. The former encourages an honest, thoughtful response based on experience; the latter asks for wishful thinking or even a little lying just to sound good.

Again, stick to what people really have done, not what they "might" do given a hypothetical scenario. The following dialogue provides a question about specific actions taken by a candidate and two possible responses:

Interviewer: We have all been in situations that test how far we should go in making a sale. Tell me about a situation in which you had to use "creative financing" to close the deal.

Candidate #1: Sure, I was working a $100K sale and my commission was going to be $10,000. My company had a "one price to all" policy, so I couldn't offer any discounts to them. The key decision maker had told me over lunch that there was this bass boat he wanted, but he couldn't get the price down. I went by the boat dealer and arranged a discount ($1,500 off) and had the dealer call my new best friend at the company. I told the decision maker about my negotiation, and he decided to buy our product. I paid the boat dealer $1,500 out of my commission, so it didn't cost my company anything.

Candidate #2: Sure, I was working a big sale with Ztech Corp. One buyer there hinted that he expected some consideration if he was going to recommend our product to the purchasing committee. I told him I couldn't give any more than a guarantee of service support after the sale and that it was our policy to offer "one price to all." I lost that sale, but we also never had a problem with other customers thinking they could somehow get a lower price. The next year we did close business with them—full price, but we did arrange time payments. Funny thing is we made almost as much money on the interest as we made on the sale.

While anyone might appreciate the creativity shown by Candidate #1, Candidate #2 got the job. Honesty and adherence to company policy, not to mention ethics, drove the decision. Here we have an example of how deep and broad behavior-based and experience-based questioning revealed a much richer picture of a candidate than would have been the case with a hypothetical scenario attempting to get at the same issues.

Chapter 9

Conduct a **Structured** Interview

IN THE PREVIOUS CHAPTER we discussed the need to use behavioral questions rather than hypothetical ones when interviewing candidates. Here we will cover (1) the key elements of a structured interview, (2) the fairest and most efficient interviewing methods, and (3) the practices least likely to create defects in the hiring process.

- In the same way as you planned the whole recruiting and hiring campaign, *you also must plan each interview.* Read over the resume and/or notes of the telephone screening. Write out questions that pertain to the person's specific experience as well as the standard questions you will ask. Include questions that directly or indirectly relate to the job accountabilities as listed in the job description. If there are company-mandated application documents, be sure to include them in the folder or notebook for the interview. Plan for each interview to run approximately one hour, with thirty minutes between interviews. Experienced managers try to limit themselves to five or fewer face-to-face interviews in a day. You need time between interviews and time to think about and compare your results at the end of the day.

- *Create a list of behavioral questions,* some that are generic and some that are specific to the individual. As an example, if your position requires managing a team, you should ask questions relevant to that skill and experience: "In your resume I saw a reference to your team leadership at Ztech Corp. Can you tell me a bit about that experience and how you handled division of labor issues and individual accountability on that team?" This kind of question speaks to a specific experience. "Tell me about a time you led a team." "What sorts of goals were set for the team to reach?" and "How did that go?" are generic to any team experience a candidate may have.

- *Remember to get at talent and ability rather than skill and experience whenever that is possible.* Logically, unless you have a goal to hire only specifically experienced people, you must get to aptitudes, innate ability, and likelihood of success, despite the candidate's lack of familiarity with specific duties of the job. This means you have to ask questions that uncover how good a person is at learning a complex task, for example, or what situations he or she succeeded in that were *similar and transferable* to the new job assignment. If you are interviewing a recent college graduate going for a first job, but you have team management as required experience, you should ask questions about teamwork in college. Many students are exposed to teamwork in classes, through extracurricular activities, and in sports.

- *Set the time and expect the candidate to be there.* Punctuality must be respected by the candidate and yourself. Tardiness may indicate lack of respect or point to organizational problems. The candidate should actually be early for an interview and the interviewer a little early or exactly on time.

- *Greet the candidate and put him or her at ease.* Tell the candidate your name and title, indicate where he or she is to sit and if any refreshments (water or coffee) are available, and briefly explain the interview process. A few minutes of small talk may also help put a candidate at ease, but don't waste time chatting.

- Some companies like to take executive candidates to lunch or dinner to check them out in a *social context.* It is in this sort of context that outside interests can be covered without detracting from the more formal structured interview. If a social venue is not appropriate or feasible and you still feel that one's broader personal interests are important for your consideration, then include such questions in your structured interview. Just beware of crossing over into personal matters that could cause you legal problems (see Chapter 10).

- If this is the very first interview, that is, there was not an informational telephone screening prior to this meeting, then you should *give a brief explanation of the company and the opportunity the person is applying for.* Rehearse this statement and hold to that information throughout the series of interviews. "I understand you are interested in our operations management position in Des Moines, right? This is a key position that involves management of seven direct reports and a liaison relationship to customer service. You are presenting yourself as a candidate for this position because of your prior experience in operations and supervision. Correct?" With this kind of scripted statement you cover all the basic prerequisites and determine the person's fit to be in the pool of viable candidates.

- Without structure, planning, and some scripting, hiring managers can get off track with some candidates and spend more time talking than listening and more time answering a candidate's questions than the other way around—they become the interviewee rather than the interviewer. *The hiring manager should spend the bulk of the interview listening.* It is a good practice to state at the beginning, "This will be a structured interview that will keep us on track and make sure we cover all of your essential experiences needed for us to make an informed decision. At the end of this part of the interview you'll have time to ask any questions you may have."

- *Verify any relevant factual information* that may be unclear to you in the application or resume. Be careful at this point to stick to areas that are relevant to the job requirements. It is illegal to ask questions such as "When did you graduate from high school?" as a means of determining age. In fact, you can't ask any questions to determine age because age discrimination is illegal. (See Chapter 10 for more information on legal issues.) If you require that the candidate have a diploma, it is fair to ask if he or she has one, of course. Even then, however, make sure that it really is a requirement of the job. One company routinely advertised for positions stating that a bachelor's degree was required for an entry-level sales position. Years later someone pointed out that the president of the company was a college dropout—a very smart dropout, to be sure, but one without a degree.

- *The heart of a structured interview with a basically prequalified candidate should last about one hour.* A well-structured interview gets at relevant detail in about this much time. More time than that can be chitchat—that's not all bad, but remember that the most relevant parts of the interview are the candidate's answers to behavioral questions. There is an unproven belief that "long interviews are better interviews." This is usually a candidate's perspective that, if the interview was scheduled to last one hour and went two, "they must really like me." In fact, the extra long interview is just as likely to be due to lack of planning and structure on the part of the hiring authority.

- *Candidates are either naturally or as a result of training reluctant to answer "negative experience" questions.* For example, if you say, "Tell me about a major mistake you made," the candidate might say, "Well, I made some minor mistakes when I was a rookie, but I have learned a lot from them." And then he or she might describe a fairly common error in his or her industry. "Yes, I overbooked us by eight rooms. Boy, was I embarrassed! But I placed all the guests nearby in upgraded rooms, and they were happy."

- On the other hand, you could say, "We have all made mistakes in this industry. One time I booked rooms for forty people from Entropy, Inc., not realizing the company was about to go bankrupt. We had a policy of checking on solvency for corporate accounts, but I didn't check. We lost about $25,000 when they bellied up and didn't pay their bill." After hearing your "confession," the candidate would be much more likely to reveal a real whopper of an error when you say, "Did you ever let something like that happen? What did you learn from it?"

- *The wrap-up should be limited to answering questions that the candidate asks.* Some interviewing authorities put a lot of emphasis on this "end game." Be aware that it may be just that—a game. Practiced interviewees may have a great store of thoughtful questions. These may be good ones, and you may appreciate the candidate's savvy, cunning, closing techniques, and thoughtfulness. If all that dovetails with a good impression created from responses to your questions, that's OK. Just keep the "close" in perspective. Sure, you want a good close, but it has to be measured in the context of the whole interview. One interviewee had a clever close: He opened his briefcase and produced a felt chalkboard eraser, which he placed in the middle of the table. He said, "I want to erase any doubt you may have that I am the right person for this job." The hiring authority shared this "clever close" with his boss, who said, "Jeez, I hadn't heard that one since the Seventies! You know he tried that with me, too!"

- At the very end, *the hiring manager should provide information on the next steps in the process.* Being somewhat noncommittal at the end of a first full structured interview is OK or even desirable if more candidates are to be seen. In any case the next steps should be conditional: "If you remain under consideration after this round of interviews, we will contact you."

In summary, a structured interview has many advantages over an open-ended, conversational interview, such as:

- You control the interview time and content.
- You keep on target with relevant subject matter.
- You are able to fairly compare several candidates for the same position because you asked the same, or very similar, questions of each applicant.

Chapter 10

Follow **Legal and Ethical Guidelines** in Hiring

IT IS VERY IMPORTANT to know the basic law when hiring. Of course, this is not only the right thing to do, but it is also the only way to avoid expensive litigation arising from discrimination lawsuits. Hiring authorities simply need to be fair. They should also *want* to be fair because diversity in a workforce is a fundamentally good idea with very positive benefits for most companies. Being fair and legal means treating all applicants alike in the hiring process. Here are the main considerations:

- The basis of equal opportunity is no discrimination toward any individual on the basis of race, religion, color, national origin, age, physical handicap, sex, marital status, change of marital status, pregnancy, or parenthood. Any interviewing questions regarding any items in the above statement might be construed as discriminatory. Avoid interviewing questions on any of those subjects. Even "subtle" or clever questions to try to determine age or ethnic origin, for example, should be avoided. For example, one might try to determine age by asking when someone graduated from high school. If you do so, you must ask every candidate that question, not just the ones that seem older than the range you are trying to hire in. More to the point, why should you care? If someone is qualified, age shouldn't matter.

- *Treat each applicant the same as every other one.* There was a case (and lawsuit) wherein one applicant, a female, had a short interview of around fifteen minutes. In another interview on the same day with a male, the interviewer asked more questions, more time was spent, and the candidate made it to the next round. These candidates both worked at the same school and knew each other well enough to get together and compare notes on their interviewing experience. The woman felt she had been discriminated against because she had better credentials, longer experience, and several more awards than the male candidate, yet was not being considered for the position. Only the positive record at the hiring company of employing many females and female managers, showing the lack of a pattern of discrimination, saved that particular company from paying a large settlement. Even a successful judgment is very expensive for a company. All of that could have been avoided by simply treating the two candidates alike.

- Stick to the positive attributes, skill, talent, and experience that pertain to the business problem or tasks and accountabilities that will confront the applicant once hired. This is safe, legal ground. When you think about it, all else is irrelevant anyway. For example, many management jobs require extensive business travel. If travel is required in the job, it would be imperative to cover this subject in an interview. This happens to be a common area of potential discrimination. It is all too easy to ask lifestyle-related questions on travel issues such as "What would your spouse think of your being away from home three nights a week?" This is a horrible way to ask! First, it is a hypothetical question presuming a potential inability or reluctance to perform a task based on an unknown factor in the candidate's personal relationship. The question is also illegal. It introduces a criterion based on marital status and an imagined, presumed negative impact that status could have on job performance. While it is easy to see why such a question may be posed, it is much better, and legal, to ask the question this way: "Is there any reason that the three days of overnight travel per week this job requires would be a problem for you?" If the candidate says, "No," you can accept that at face value and/or probe further with questions about real experience in traveling. "All of us who travel for a living have some negative experiences about that aspect of the job. Tell me how you have coped with traveling three or four days out of every week." This line of questioning is fair, legal, and gets to the information wanted.

- Earlier it was stressed that you *use the same set of behavioral questions in each structured interview.* Not only does this method give you the best way to compare candidates, but it is also the fairest and most legally defensible way to avoid any claims of discrimination.

Finally, and perhaps most importantly, the hiring manager must buy-in to the concept that hiring for diversity is a very positive thing. Any organization, large or small, can and will benefit by having different types of people working together. Variety of experience and outlook can broaden the scope and success of the organization. The very fact that people are different is a strength in most organizations.

Chapter 11

Sell the Company to the Candidate

IN RECENT YEARS, a low unemployment rate, even in so-called periods of economic slowdown, has made the market for skilled and talented employees very tight. Jobs are going unfilled because there are simply more jobs than there are candidates to fill them. The demographics, with the Baby Boomers beginning to reach retirement in the next few years, show this trend will continue for the foreseeable future. It is thus somewhat surprising that hiring authorities at many companies fail to realize that they are in competition for the most talented people. Some even take an arrogant attitude: "We are great; if a fool turns us down, that's OK!" After the first couple of interviews, when it becomes clear a finalist is in sight and the hiring manager has done the qualifying and selection screening, he or she now needs to do some selling.

Consider this:

- *You must create desire on the part of the candidate to work for you.* Just as you would do if you were selling your product to a customer, you should see the interview as your opportunity for a sales presentation. The best hires want to work for a company not just for the money, but for the challenge, growth, and satisfaction of being in an organization they admire.

- *Sell the candidate on the big picture.* Why should he or she work at your company rather than another? Does the company have a vision statement—what does this mean? What is the word on the street about your company—good rumors as well as bad? Not only do you want to make sure that candidates feel good and have the right information, but you also want to dispel any anxiety they might have. One manager said, "There's nothing to that buy-out rumor" when an official announcement on a merger was made that very day. The disenchanted candidate turned down the offer. This was a sad outcome because there was, in fact, a very positive spin to the takeover—revitalization, more capital, likely expansion, and so on.

- *Uncover needs the same as you would in a sales situation.* What does the candidate really want? MRI data on thousands of candidates show that more money is not the greatest pull to change jobs or launch a new career. These days, lifestyle and family issues such as housing and schools can be of greater importance. One small company, located in a medium-sized Midwestern town, was very successful competing for employee talent against major Northeastern competitors. They offered membership in the local country club, with its Jack Nicklaus–designed golf course, and sold the benefits of living in a typical family town with a nationally ranked school system.

• *Finding "hot buttons" (issues that motivate a person, positively or negatively) is not only good selling, but it can save the company money,* too. Learning what the key motivations for change are can be straightforward or subtle and indirect. "Were you satisfied with the benefits package at your previous employer?" and "What did you like or not like about it?" are direct questions that may raise an issue that can be exploited in introducing your benefits package. Asking, "What are the most important factors to you in making the decision to come to our company?" is a more open-ended approach. Here's an indirect way to uncover hot buttons: "While money is important, what do you think motivates people to change jobs?" If you assume that giving someone a fat raise is all that's needed for him or her to come over to your company, you might be making a costly mistake. Maybe it's having a better office, a better car, or a company child day-care center that will appeal to this particular candidate. Who knows if you don't ask? One company offered a whopping 20 percent sign-on bonus that was not asked for, but failed to mention the standard week off between Christmas and New Year's, which would have closed the hire without any sign-on money.

- *Don't be passive or casual about the hiring offer.* Again, treat the process the same way you would a major sale. After all, won't this hire be just as important to your bottom line as any big sale? Some companies let events in the hiring process just slide along with a reactive, go-with-the-flow mentality. They tolerate behaviors in hiring that would never be allowed in selling or customer service situations. For example, failing to call a candidate back with information, updates, or a simple explanation of a delay in the process can cause the candidate to decline an offer or accept one from a more proactive employer. Once a key HR person who had to process some final pre-hire paperwork was hospitalized for a week. No one bothered to let the candidate know, calls were not returned, and the candidate assumed lack of interest and took another offer.

- *Candidates view the hiring process as an indication of the future of working for that company.* If the process appears drawn out, overly bureaucratic, not methodical, and unresponsive to the candidate, the conclusion could be "I don't know if I want to work with them." By contrast, a well-run, relatively short process shows positive images of the company—one that a candidate should want to work for.

- *Be honest about the problems as well as the prospects for the company and the hiring position.* The truth of a negative public relations situation will probably come out. It is better to be in control by anticipating that the candidate will raise the issue. One manufacturing firm was involved in a massive product recall that nearly brought it down. Fortunately for the company, the forthright managers were able to address the issues head-on and managed to keep hiring good people in the face of adversity. They put the negative issue behind them, showed what corrective steps had been taken, and made the prospective hires feel that they were part of a new team with a clean slate.

- Most importantly, *sell the business need for the position.* It is very important to establish, from the very beginning conversation, a clear business objective for hiring. This goes beyond the job description into immediate issues and goals, both short-term and long-term. After all, people are hired in a profit-centered business to help the business reach its profit goals. Be sure to let the candidate know what is expected in that regard.

- Last, *it is important that the hiring manager keep control of the process* as much as possible. Control slips away, for example, when candidates begin to lose interest in the opportunity or want more compensation than you want to pay. Control, in this context, means you hold (or are perceived to hold) the cards the candidate wants, both in the opportunity and in the compensation package. The hiring manager may not actually control the budget, for example, but should be regarded as the person having authority to convey the offer.

You cannot assume that the person is "buying" any of this unless you do a great job of selling yourself and the company. In the context of selling the position to the buying candidate, the hiring manager should be perceived as the one in control: the one who can be relied on to provide information, answer questions, and make the offer.

Chapter 12

Red Flags in the Process **Cannot Be Ignored**

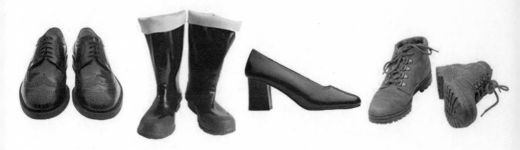

THE TIME SPENT IN COMMUNICATING with an applicant is brief. The opportunity to observe behavior is limited to the artificial environment of the face-to-face interview and a few phone calls. A "red flag" in this context is any negative behavior, however small, that shows up prior to an offer being made.

Think of your close observation as a lens through which you as the hiring manager can augment your microcosmic view. This can help the filtering process by allowing you to see another side of the candidate more clearly. We'll talk about tests and other screening devices later. Right now, we'll look at red flags—both small and large—that may emerge to disqualify an applicant and how to deal with them.

- *Even a small negative issue should be examined* in the decision process. For example, let's say a candidate is

late for the appointment. Some managers may disqualify any candidate who shows up so much as a
minute late—no excuses! Tardiness is a red flag, and if
it is in the context of an interview it is a very serious
matter. If you do accept an excuse, it had better be a
good one: "I was stuck in traffic" is not a good
excuse—the candidate should have anticipated that
and planned to arrive on time despite traffic. "My car
was hijacked," on the other hand, is a pretty good
excuse, but only if the candidate calls to tell you right
after calling the police.

- *Vague answers usually mean a cover-up.* Here the red flag
  is either poor memory or poor results. People do not
  easily forget their achievements, but they will change
  the subject, answer with "I don't recall," or be otherwise evasive when they are not proud of the truth. If
  you say, "Our experience shows that strong college
  performers seem to do better in learning technical
  material required in selling this product. Was your
  GPA high?" "How high?" the candidate might ask.
  "We look for at least 3.0 or the equivalent. It could be a
  little lower if you worked your way through college."
  "Gosh, I can't remember what mine was," the candidate says, not because he or she really doesn't know,
  but because he or she really wasn't a B student. The
  same thing applies to sales achievements: Anyone who
  has a solid record knows pretty much exactly what it
  was. In many occupations, competitive metrics count a
  great deal in job performance. Such numbers as call
  quantity, quality control of defect percentage, amount

of production, or other measurable results are counted to document productivity. These results are usually very well-known to those who are high achievers. The other side is that these numbers are often forgotten by those whose achievements were less admirable.

- *Good communication during the process predicts good communication after the hire.* Missed calls, excessive phone tag, and failure to call back are all signs that a person is just not as communicative as most managers expect their employees to be. Especially if the position you are hiring for is remote from the office or daily contact, you would want to make sure the person to be hired is an excellent and regular communicator. After the first interview, you might say, "After our meeting today, give me your thoughts about the job in an e-mail to me." A serious candidate will take this as an order and return a message at his or her earliest convenience. Not only can you determine interest in the job, but you can get a snapshot of future communication with that individual. A candidate who fails to pick up on the significance of your request for follow-up will likely be a non-communicator in the future.

- *Preparation for the interview is a good predictor of planning skills and style.* Ask, "So what did you do to get ready for this interview?" A good response would include coming with questions and doing at least a little research on the company. Lacking this sort of preparation, how well do you think the candidate would plan his or her work once hired? Many managers rightly expect the candidates to have been to the company website. You will have the opportunity not only to see what their impressions are, but also to what extent they have any creative, insightful, or analytical ideas about your company. If you are interviewing for a product manager, you might be very specific in probing for the impressions one has from what he or she has seen at the site. For a finance position, ask what the person thinks of the statements available from web-based information. Stop and think: What sort of person, coming for an interview, would not do this kind of basic preparation? Someone you want on your team?

- *Even something as intangible as "energy level" can be determined* by asking the right questions and observing the candidate's behavior. "This position involves a lot of walking and time standing. Tell me about some of your recreational activities over the past several weeks." If a person says he or she has done nothing because there's no time, that could mean low energy. Energetic people are usually involved in activities that require energy. Do they have to run marathons? Of course not. Even sedentary activities like playing bridge or chess, especially if it's a regular activity, are good signs of an energetic person. Good posture, attentiveness, and a quick sense of humor are all signs of a higher energy level.

- *Try to separate hyperbole from lying.* Salespeople tend to exaggerate their successes and minimize their failures. Statements with very round numbers, such as, "I had a million-dollar increase in sales" are somewhat suspect, whereas exact information, such as, "My increase in 2002 was $973,000" is more likely to be accurate and can be verified with a document. If the person had one penny over a million, he or she might say, "My increase was over a million." Is this significant? Maybe, maybe not. Look for patterns. If the same person who slightly inflated performance results also says something like, "I worked night and day for two weeks on that assignment," you may begin to wonder where the hyperbole ends and lying begins. That's your red flag.

- *Avoidance of specifics in recalling experience is a red flag.* Listen for answers that are generalities when you asked for specifics: "I usually try to talk to twenty or thirty clients a day" is rather vague, whereas the following is very specific: "My plan calls for seeing and or talking to thirty clients a day, and I regularly do that. My worst day was twenty-two a month ago, during a flood, but I offset that with a forty-two-call day last Thursday. I have a plan book on my computer planner to track this."

- *Delays in accepting an offer are usually red flags.* If a person has been interviewing for several weeks and you finally make an offer, but then the candidate has to "think it over," what does this say about commitment, interest, motivation, et cetera? Is he or she still trying to decide whether to take the job? Is he or she unhappy with the terms of the offer? Does he or she expect a counteroffer from a current employer? Of course, if a relocation is involved or if the hiring process developed suddenly and moved very rapidly, a solid candidate may indeed need a little time to weigh the offer and everything a job change means. Considering that, remember that the most motivated and committed candidate will be ready to accept a reasonable offer (usually discussed prior to the actual offer) at the time that offer is made. Twenty-four hours is the standard for acceptance of an offer. Think about withdrawing an offer if a candidate cannot commit within that period.

- *Eliminate false red flags by probing.* Sometimes red flags are actually checkered flags—the flag of a winner—due to simple misunderstanding of facts.

Once a young man, we'll call him "Ralph," was coming to a company for a second round of interviews. The hiring manager was watching as Ralph crossed the parking lot on a cold, dark winter morning. The manager noticed the candidate made an abrupt turn and backtracked to a new Porsche 911 parked with the lights on. He saw the young man open the door and turn off the lights. Ralph then proceeded to the building for the interview. The hiring manager was colder in his attitude than he had been before. He recalled that early on Ralph had spoken of earning his way through school working nights and weekends. He said, "Ralph, tell me again about how your parents lacked money to send you to school and how you had to work hard for everything you have today."

"That's right. Sometimes I actually went without food. I worked at least forty hours a week throughout the year."

"We'll be in touch," said the manager as he closed the interview and sent Ralph on his way. "By the way, I like

your car, had one myself—good German engineering!"
Ralph grinned and said, "Yes, it is reliable!"

Ralph, the supposed fabricator, not a rich kid whose parents sent him to school or bought him that $70,000 car, went out to the lot, got in his ten-year-old Volkswagen and drove off, never getting the job. The good Samaritan who turned out some rich guy's Porsche lights did go on to great things, and the manager who failed to follow up on his concern missed out on an opportunity to hire a good employee.

Increase Your Knowledge of the Candidate Through **Tests, Trials, Role Plays, and Projects**

EMPLOYERS MAY USE TESTING AS PART of the selection process. It is often a matter of policy whether or not various tests are used. Generally speaking, testing is a good idea because it does correlate with elimination of the wrong people while emphasizing qualities of better fit hires. *Testing* is both a generic and a specific term, taking several forms that go beyond interviewing to determine a candidate's fit for a given position. Here are examples of testing in the trial sense:

- Any *trial run at the position*, such as a day on the job with a hiring manager, is one kind of test. For specific skilled positions, such as air traffic controller, the idea of doing the job for a few hours to demonstrate competence would be an appropriate test. One company hiring a mid-management pressroom supervisor had all candidates actually operate the press for a day. Not only did this demonstrate necessary skill, but it showed that the candidate was not above the hands-on work to be supervised, a shared value throughout that organization.

Some sales managers like to take prospective sales-people on real calls as observers. "What did you see going on with the client on that last call? Did you observe any hidden objections or buying signals?" Again, this a test of an ability that would be called for in a particular job. Again, consistency is called for. Any hurdle created for one candidate should apply to all peers in the same pool of candidates. One hiring manager feared (with prejudice) that a rather obese candidate would not perform well in an outside sales position. He required a full day working with a current rep on a physically demanding schedule. In this case, the apparently physically challenged person ran circles around the manager. Justifiably so, that person was offered the job. But what if this physical trial were not part of the process for others with similar qualifications? What if those who appeared fit were not given the same test? And then the person who did all the sweating was eliminated? This could be the basis of a lawsuit. It would have been better simply to ask about physically demanding activities performed in the past and make a judgment based on the answers.

- *Role playing* may suffice as a competence test as well, especially where skills and talent are less easily demonstrated in a real context. Retail buyers must negotiate with vendors daily, so, for example, a scenario with roles for "buyer" and "vendor" could be easily devised to demonstrate negotiating talent. Role plays can show a person in action. If someone applies for an entry-level sales job, he or she may have no sales or negotiating experience. If you want to test sales aptitude, you may have candidates role play selling a product to you. Do they ask questions to determine need? Do they match benefits to needs? Do they close? For the most part, entry-level people who can do that much probably do have sales savvy despite lack of experience.

- *Remember the advantages of behavioral and experience-based interviewing, and avoid hypothetical testing* as well. Sure, a role play can be made up, but it should be a composite of realistic situations. So don't just ask, "What would you do?" or "Imagine this hypothetical situation." Instead say, "Based on your experience, take this case and suggest a solution." Follow up with, "Does that situation seem familiar from your own experience? Tell me about that problem and how you solved it."

- An *in-basket problem,* where a sheaf of typical memos and reports is given to a candidate for a management position to analyze and prioritize, constitutes another type of trial or test. "Given this information, what would you do first and why?" Design the trial project to be as real as possible. A prospective marketing manager might be given an in-basket budget problem—all the variables of spending options, product description, market research data, and so on—in a folder with the assignment: "Take a look at this material, think about it, and tell me your budget allocation. You'll have two hours to review the material and write a brief paragraph on your recommendations." If this activity resembles the job that person would be asked to do, it could be a useful tool in evaluating the candidate. But if the task does not really resemble actual tasks for the job, it may just be a waste of everyone's time.

- As with structured interviewing, when conducting trials or competence tests, role plays, or pre-hire tasks, *the key is to be consistent.* If you require one candidate in the pool to do any of the assignments, require all to do the same or a very similar task.

Next we'll look at formal testing—the commercially available psychological, aptitude, or intelligence tests used to measure and compare individuals. Hiring managers who don't use pre-employment testing in their hiring processes cite a number of reasons for their decisions. The most common objections we hear are based on myth instead of reality. These include (1) a candidate might sue us, (2) it is too expensive, (3) it is too time-consuming, and (4) testing doesn't really work. Here are some points about formal tests and testing services:

- *Integrating pre-employment testing into your hiring process can increase retention and productivity,* as well as decrease the likelihood of employment practices lawsuits. The important thing is to be consistent. Treat each pool of candidates as similarly as you can, and there will be no problem with lawsuits based on dis-crimination. If everyone in the pool is tested, no one can say he or she was singled out for testing.

- Most tests are available for less than $500. If you can batch purchase or subscribe to a certain periodic usage, you can probably receive even better pricing.

- *SelecSys*™ and *Caliper* are both well-established testing programs that address the last two points very well. Tests can be administered and scored electronically in less than a hour. As far as reliability is concerned, ask the managers who use these devices—they will tell you that there is a high degree of correlation between certain scores and profile patterns and future performance in certain occupations. The reliability of these tests is their main selling point. The main proof is that companies continue to buy them.

- Several personality tests are available that *profile people best fit for certain careers.* While none of these tests is infallible, aptitude tests can shed light on some aspects of personality. For example, most of the commercial tests can reveal traits such as impatience. In some positions—for example, customer service—that may be a negative attribute, but it might be perceived as a strength in production line management.

- *Never use a test as the sole indicator or predictor of fit for a particular position.* Even if it can be demonstrated that the better tests turn up potential weaknesses and strengths, it is best to follow up with interviewing questions that probe deeper into those traits.

- Both *SelecSys*™ and *Wonderlic*® are popular tests for management and sales positions. Bigby Havis & Associates, Inc., and Bartell & Bartell Ltd. are two major consulting firms that offer on-line testing for executive level positions.

- *Make sure that the test has some reputation for validity and reliability* (the above mentioned ones do). The best "test of the test" for your given circumstances is the extent to which successful people in your organization achieve the results the test says are indicators of success in their particular fields. If you are instituting a new test, take it yourself and give it to your colleagues. The results can be informative, or at least entertaining!

- Be sure to *understand what the results of testing say.* All of the standard, commercially available tests have a good deal of interpretive material and guidelines. In larger companies, an HR department may handle both the administration and interpretation of tests. Make sure that someone is responsible for providing the summary of what the test means.

If tests and trials are not used consistently, defects will be introduced into the hiring process. For example, one company had two candidates from other industries. After talking about the differences in the work environment, they assigned a project that would give a candidate the experience of a typical day on the job. Because another candidate in the same pool had no time for this project, the assignment was waived for that candidate. The first candidate did not have great success with the trial day, but at least did something. The second candidate actually looked better overall for having done nothing with a trial day project and was eventually hired. Not only was this unfair to the first candidate, but the company also created a defect in its process by not insisting that the second candidate perform the same task. The company took an unnecessary chance in finding out more about the fit of the candidate *after* the person was on the payroll.

Chapter **14**

Always Check **References**

REFERENCE CHECKING is used to verify truly qualified finalists for a position. Failure to check references can be a huge defect in the hiring process. There have been cases of people who did not exist getting jobs! One seemingly perfect candidate claimed honors graduation from a first-class college as well as a fantastic award-winning sales record and listed some well-known local businesspeople as references. He was actually a fugitive from a felony conviction whose entire resume, name and all, was fabricated. References were not verified, and the crook was hired and promptly disappeared with the company car.

The main points in the reference checking process are these:

- *Clear the process with the candidate* and use a list provided by him or her. While permission is tacitly granted by listing names of references, getting a candidate to sign off on a list of people who will actually be contacted is a good idea. Any hesitancy on the candidate's part to provide a list of references or reluctance to permit a reference check should be a cause for concern.

- *The reference list should primarily contain business associates, former supervisors, and customers.* Everybody has a friend, preacher, or neighbor who will say something nice, but business contacts matter the most. Sometimes companies are reluctant to make calls to check references; after all, the contacts may be their competitors and customers. This is an area where using a professional recruiter provides a great advantage. Whether it is psychological or just one degree of separation, a recruiter who is working with an individual known to the reference contact has a better chance of finding out detailed information. This is not to say that you can't get a good reference; it's just more difficult and less likely to contain depth of information. That's OK if all you really need is verification of employment.

- Your approach to reference checking should be *as thorough as your approach to a telephone screening* interview with a candidate. You may not be able to get at all the information you want, but try. (An excellent form to use for this purpose is found in Appendix B.)

- *Use reference checking to find out more about the candidate as a person*—not just the facts, but also the opinions others hold about that person as an employee and associate. "Tell me what management style would you say he (or she) used in supervising employees? Closer to hands-on micromanagement or was she (or he) more of a strategic manager, less involved in the day-to-day?" These are leading questions used to draw the person out and get more information than the bare facts.

- *Many former employers are reluctant (or forbidden by policy) to say very much about a former employee* beyond verifying dates of employment. However, anyone listed as a reference by a candidate was, presumably, alerted by him or her to provide information to a hiring authority. It is a red flag if a person listed as a reference refuses to discuss the candidate's qualifications.

- *Many people will put names on a reference list with the thought that references are often not checked*—and, unfortunately, they are right. Many, if not most, companies do little, if any, reference checking. One applicant claimed to have been "Rep of the Year" with a certain firm in Michigan. He listed his former boss as a reference. That person was called for a verification of performance and said, "Who? Oh, yeah, he was here a while. Rep of the Year? No. He definitely wasn't Rep of the Year. He quit just before being fired for nonperformance." Needless to say, that candidate was not hired.

- *Thorough reference checking can give you great insight on the performance of the candidate.* By asking penetrating questions, you can even determine management issues that may predict the person's future success in the position. For example, you may want an individual to be very independent, a self-starter, or work with minimal supervision. Ask questions that bring this out. Or perhaps you have a team environment. Ask, "How do you think Mary would work out on a management team?" One reference may say, "Gee, she is kind of a maverick—that's what I liked about her!" Would you have the same opinion if you were depending on Mary to work with others to carry out your policy? That is something to think about. Carry this thought into the next reference check. If you have a doubt, you may have a red flag situation, or the issue could be completely cleared up: "Well, I wouldn't say she was a 'maverick'—she was the one who generally saw things a little bit differently. She challenged the team she was on to consider alternatives. I guess that's why her team came in over goal and under budget!"

- Since conducting the reference interview takes more time than mere fact checking, be sure to *say up-front that you may need twenty minutes to half an hour* and set an appointment for a later call if necessary.

Reference checking is one of the hiring activities the hiring manager must either do or delegate to a reliable recruiter or to the HR department. Beyond the basics of verifying facts such as dates of employment, it is a good idea to gain as much insight as you can by asking good questions of the person providing the reference.

Chapter 15

Share Decisions on Hiring

IT IS A VERY GOOD PRACTICE to involve others in the hiring process, even if you are the top person in the company hiring your Number Two. Obtaining more opinions reduces hiring errors, as long as the process is under control and input is sought for specific purposes. *Advice* from a small, diverse group is more important in the decision process than a vote for or against a candidate. Keep the following in mind:

- *Ask for feedback from all persons who talked to the candidates*—even the receptionist, who might have observed the candidate waiting and may have some interesting insights. Some of the best reality checks in the process are the discussions you have with your colleagues. You should regard any disagreements about a candidate's qualifications or fit as potential red flags about that person.

- *Others in the company will have different points of view.* The other perspectives may uncover problems or discover strengths in the candidate that you overlooked. For example, one candidate was thought "too mild-mannered for the dynamics of marketing" by the hiring manager. Another interviewer uncovered that he actually had been a drill sergeant in the U.S. Marines. After learning that, the hiring manager had an impression of "quiet strength" and certainly had no thoughts of that candidate not being assertive enough.

- *Consider the politics of your committee.* What power and position issues are at work in a given committee chosen to accomplish a given purpose. The truth is that human resource department personnel do not have the same stake as those directly involved in generating profits. This is not a slam on HR—these departments handle many of the company's issues, benefits, and training— but, again, they are not the managers directly charged with either making or saving the company money. A marketing manager on the committee to select a manager in product development may have input on the communication skills of a candidate with an engineering background. That candidate's engineering skills may be more important, however, so marketing's vote may not weigh as heavily in the decision. Certainly, if it were uncovered that a strong production engineer candidate did possess good communication skills, that candidate's chances should be excellent for being hired.

- *Some fear that "hiring by committee" is not a good idea,* as committees tend toward conservative inaction that drags the process out ad infinitum. This happens when the hiring committee is set up in the wrong way. Instead of selecting the committee for negative (or positive) feedback, *select members for narrowly defined purposes.* For example, from two to five other people are invited to the committee to cover specific aspects of the opportunity by functional areas: One person may concentrate on management crises faced by the candidate; another, perhaps a future peer, would deal with teamwork experience; and so on. Without instruction or defined guidelines, a committee tends to be more like an inquisition, looking for any sign of heresy to eliminate the candidate from consideration.

  Another way to set up a committee is vertically, with members drawn from future peers, reports, and another manager at the same level as the hiring manager. Thus you gain insight into how a person relates to people he or she may report to, people who will report to him or her, and equals he or she may work with daily.

- *Any disagreement as to the fit of the person for the job should be regarded as a red flag.* Of course, reasonable people do disagree, but misgivings should be aired and resolved before going further. Once a candidate stated on a resume and in the course of her interviews that she had had a "sales training course at Columbia University in New York City." This claim surprised the hiring manager who, familiar with the prestigious institution, doubted that Columbia offered such a course. It turned out she had been sent to a building owned by Columbia University but rented to her former employer, and there she had taken a training seminar. Technically speaking, she wasn't lying—just puffing something up. One manager discussed the incident with another. They disagreed over the importance of this little issue: One thought it showed "creativity"; the other saw it as a lie. She was hired, and guess what? She frequently lied about sales prospects, the number of contacts, and her whereabouts for whole days at a time. This eventually led to a nasty termination and the loss of many sales opportunities.

- *Do not grant a veto unless it is the CEO with that power.* While it is important to recognize differences of opinion, the hiring manager should not lean so far to accommodate others in the decision process that the effect of disagreement is a veto. One person giving feedback on an interview was alarmed that a candidate had asked what type shoes she should wear. The candidate came from a company that required women to wear heels. The hiring company not only had no such policy, but the interviewer did not know why such a question would be asked and thought that the subject of footwear was trivial. The conclusion of that particular committee member was that the candidate had no substantive questions other than what sort of shoes to wear. She recommended not hiring that candidate. The hiring authority did not probe further, took the recommendation as a veto, and might have made a bad decision as a result. The point is, take a disagreement as a red flag and resolve that issue. If a misunderstanding or factual misinformation is at the root of the disagreement, make sure the person raising the issue understands that. If the person's point is valid, then reconsider whether you want to hire the candidate.

- *Make sure other hiring managers read this book* or at least understand the principles and practices of *Zero Defect Hiring.* It makes little sense to follow the best practices outlined here if others involved in the hiring process do not know or understand them.

Using committee input in the decision-making process can improve chances of making a good hiring decision. However, the hiring manager must ultimately make the decision. Most companies include hiring authority among key accountabilities of their mid-level managers. A committee can help with the decision, but it comes down to you.

Chapter 16

Act with a Sense of **Urgency**

EVEN THOUGH HIRING to a deadline is not a good practice, hiring with an open-ended schedule is dangerous as well. For one thing, excellent candidates do not keep forever. Remember, you are in competition for talent. A hiring decision should be at least on the same plane of urgency as your major contracts, perhaps of higher importance than any one of them. Here are some thoughts on the subject of urgency:

- Sometimes, when the general economy is in a down-turn, it can seem to a company or hiring manager that there are unlimited human resources to draw from. The problem is that this thinking lulls you into a false sense of security. You believe there is a veritable horde of outstanding people laid off and on the job market that you can draw on at a moment's notice. *The reality is that there are very low percentages of unemployed people in the United States and most other first-world economies.* According to MRI, the world's largest executive staffing firm, unemployment has been under 5 percent for the universe of middle-income working people in most industrialized countries. In management positions the unemployment rate rarely exceeds 1 percent.

- The fact is, *the best candidates for any job are always rare.* Most of these people are not even active candidates to change jobs. The passive candidate is content where he or she is until becoming actively interested in a new opportunity. Recruiting means going after the best candidates no matter where they may be— employed, unemployed, or just starting out from college.

- *Time kills all deals.* Given enough time, anything can (and will) go wrong. The very act of delaying a process can present an image of your company as overly bureaucratic, too conservative, and unable to make decisions. It can make the hiring authority look weak or indecisive.

- *Deal-killing alternatives for a candidate, such as counter-offers, can emerge.* This is more likely to happen with an extended hiring process. Closing while the iron is hot is just as true in hiring as it is in selling a product or service.

- It is very important to *keep communicating with the candidate throughout the hiring process.* Continually seek out and respond to even small objections or questions that may arise. Some candidates are reluctant to raise concerns because they fear rejection if they press for something like a relocation allowance. The company may have a great package that wasn't been revealed to the candidate; it is better to communicate on any matter before making an offer.

- *The opportunity costs of delaying a hiring decision are great.* Companies, unfortunately, rarely assess the hidden costs associated with lost revenue due to open positions. More costs are attributed to length of time spent by hiring managers on the hiring process—a great investment of time and money that takes away from the other functions of the person's job. One company actually thought it was wise to "save" on the position salary for a couple of months. This amounted to about $24,000 in salary and benefits. Meanwhile, by its own accounting, $160,000 was lost in a revenue stream from that position. By this one measure alone, the opportunity cost was $136,000!

- *Companies sometimes bury or ignore the opportunity cost issue* by delegating the work of the open position to other people, usually peer-level employees and managers. If extended long enough, the number of open positions grows as resentful or overworked employees leave. Now there is collateral damage to deal with, adding to the cost impact of delay.

- *The best practice is to have a short, reasonable time frame in which to hire.* If you find a person qualified for the position who meets your needs, hire him or her! If you don't make the deadline, fine. Don't accept an "also ran" just to make the deadline, but remember the considerations discussed here—and continue the urgent pursuit of the right-fit hire.

Chapter 17

Negotiate Terms and **Make an Offer**

SOME GREAT RECRUITING AND HIRING EFFORT is for naught because the deal falls apart when the offer is made. You must get the compensation and benefit issues out on the table before making an offer. Here are some key considerations:

- *Negotiate the acceptable terms before making the actual offer.* It is always a good idea to float the terms of salary, bonus potential, and benefits before setting the terms down in a final offer and hire letter. This discussion may come as early as the first interview. In many cases, the salary range is part of the initial posting, as is an outline of the benefits program. "Mary, before we go further with our discussion, I want to make sure we are on the same page as far as the compensation package goes." You can ask what her expectations are. Most people are looking for the high end of the salary range if they know what that is. A responsible manager has to keep not only to budget, but also to fair pay, comparable to that paid to others in the same position, adjusted for experience. One hopes that you and Mary will not be far apart. While anything is negotiable, there usually are firm guidelines from the company side, and every individual has minimum acceptable pay standards as well. It pays to find out what those are before making a final offer and finding out that someone cannot live with it.

- A good rule of thumb is to expect to *offer a compensation package that is 10 to 15 percent above the person's last job.* Continuing surveys within major recruiting firms show that this is the norm. Twenty years ago, when the United States was in a period of double-digit inflation, the typical increase expected and given was closer to 20 percent. For the past several years low inflation has driven down the increase percentage given by most companies. Unfortunately for companies, the expectation of the 20 percent increase remains with many candidates seeking a job change. Because people normally expect a job change to be a promotion or upward career move, naturally they expect better compensation. Typically, the hiring manager (or outside recruiter) can start with the company standard pay range. Simply say, "Given your experience, does $62,000 sound about right as base salary?" If the candidate agrees, you are just about done. If not, say, "What were you expecting? $62,000 is at the senior level with our company. In looking at your past compensation, I see that $62,000 is about a 12 percent increase. I might be able to get a little more; if not, what is the minimum you will accept?" If the person says, "I want $65,000," you say: "So if I can only get you $63,000, will you reject our offer?" In this way, you establish the true "walk-away" minimum acceptable offer.

- *Don't forget "total compensation" issues, including benefits.* Once a very high-level deal fell through when the candidate balked at a Cadillac as a company car. He wanted a Mercedes. The company agreed (after much discussion). Then the candidate was unhappy that it wasn't a top-of-the line Mercedes. The offer was completely withdrawn at that point, even though less than $100 per month separated the parties on the cost of the lease. In this case, it might have been better to have laid out all of the compensation package early on, with set-asides for car allowance without specifying make and model.

- Many individuals want 20 to 30 percent more largely because they have heard about someone at the new company who made that. This is not surprising, since, *of all things that people lie about in resumes and in conversation about themselves, pay is the most commonly exaggerated.* People tend to roll all compensation into the pay line as if it were salary. They may hope no one probes for a breakdown. Another interesting take is to determine the candidate's average income for several years. There could be a recent bonus for an extraordinary performance that was far above the norm and he or she is including that in the base. No new company should be paying the bonus of an old company, but that's what happens when a salary is paid that matches income that included a big bonus.

- *A professional recruiter can negotiate very well as a middle-man.* Many companies choose to use the good offices of the recruiter because a third party carries no baggage and can clearly articulate the positions of both the candidate and the company. As matchmakers, it is the recruiter's job to bring parties together. Once a trusted relationship is established with a recruiter, it is often the recruiter who takes the company's position and terms to the candidate and either floats or makes the final offer.

- *Once you are at the point of decision, make the offer.* The best people will not tolerate much waiting. Sometimes companies are so driven by their own timetables they fail to understand that the best-qualified people do not have to wait, as they are already pursuing their decision to go for better opportunities in a new career. Too many times a company will institute a hiring freeze or want to wait for a new fiscal period before hiring, even when the clear choice hire is right in front of them. Lost opportunity is one of the greatest opportunity costs!

  These issues can be avoided by planning, but if a delay is unavoidable due to budget and policy considerations, make sure the candidate knows and understands why decisions are on hold or delayed. A reasonable explanation can buy some time. You should also make sure the candidate is willing to wait. Simply ask about the candidate's attitude toward waiting.

- *Negotiate the start date.* As obvious as this may seem to a hiring manager, there are often misunderstandings about the start date. Sometimes the former employer will expect two weeks' notice. This is not often the case where the new employer is a direct competitor of the old one. However, this is an example of where misunderstandings can arise.

- *Another issue that often comes up is vacation timing.* A good many people like to take some time off between jobs. Sometimes this is a good thing: The new hire begins the new job fresh. On the other hand, some hiring managers are put off by any discussion about vacations when they are trying to get someone to work. Anticipating a negative reaction, candidates are naturally reluctant to bring this issue up early in the interviewing process. The point here is to put these issues out on the table as you discuss terms of hire, benefits, and start date.

- *Health insurance is a very big issue these days.* If you are hiring for a big corporation, you probably offer the full menu of benefits, including a great health insurance package. It is a different story with a smaller company. You may have to offer supplemental insurance, an employee-paid plan, or perhaps a bit more pay to offset a new hire's lack of insurance. One employer found it a lot easier and less expensive for the company and the employee to go for individual rather than group health insurance plans.

- *Minimize differences in compensation by breaking them down into smaller units* of costs or income. Let's say

$2,000 of annual salary offered, or as much as needed to offset insurance costs, was all that separated your company from the acceptance of the prospective hire. Divide that amount into weekly or daily amounts: "So you are saying that if you had $8.00 more a day you would accept, but you wouldn't otherwise? After taxes, that's only about $5.00, right? We are talking about less than 2 percent, and we're offering a 12 percent increase from your former job."

- *Don't forget other benefits that might make a difference.* One recent hire was almost lost because the candidate misunderstood the company car policy. This benefit was so understated by the hiring manager that the candidate, a recent college graduate, didn't realize that he actually could keep and drive a car daily, even on personal business. The American Automobile Association rates the average costs of owning and operating an average car at more than $7,500 a year. Another person could be impressed by a free parking benefit, especially if she is accustomed to paying $25 per day!

- *Creativity can close gaps.* Most companies, especially big ones, have salary and compensation guidelines. Fairness dictates that anyone doing similar work with similar experience should be paid at about the same rate. While it is good to have a salary matrix or standard scale, it can make it difficult to hire in a competitive marketplace. Hiring someone from a direct competitor for a lateral move to your organization is really tough since the hire will expect a fairly substantial increase.

One way around this is to be creative with exceptions to the standard, such as offering a hiring bonus, to compensate for a perceived shortfall in the salary offer. This kind of pay also bridges the hire to an earned bonus payout period. Finally, by being outside the matrix, a hiring bonus does not affect salary guidelines.

Zero defect hiring means managing the whole process from inception to conclusion. It means doing a better job on all phases, beginning with planning, moving through the interview stage, and ultimately succeeding with acceptance of an offer. It means that the company brings in a productive employee with the highest prospects of success and that the newly hired employee sees a bright future ahead in a challenging and rewarding career.

Appendix **A**

Resume Comparison

THIS APPENDIX CONTAINS COMPOSITE RESUMES from two fictional people with similar backgrounds and experience. One of the resumes, O'Day's, is superior to the other for the following reasons:

- O'Day has an "objective" statement that sets the tone.

- Knight leaves out the area code for his phone number. Careless with detail?

- O'Day is consistent with detail in responsibilities and accomplishments. He lists specific accomplishments, all of which are impressive. This gives the hiring manager a very clear set of facts to check with references. Knight's contains trivia and technical jargon, which may or may not be relevant to a position for which he is applying. Nearly everyone in a mid-management position has been on a committee, so why list that if it is not special? On the other hand, if that particular committee was pivotal in the success of the company, then the resume needs to say so.

- O'Day's experience is delineated month-by-month. His overlapping work dates with obtaining a master's degree could be a positive point on capacity for work. What about Knight's rounded-off years and the potential gap in employment from 1996 to 1997? Looks like he stopped working for one company sometime in 1996 and began sometime in 1997 with the other. This may or may not be an issue. If he were hired by ZTech on December 15, 1996, with a January 1, 1997, start date, no problem.

- Knight gives no date for college graduation. Although a hiring manager cannot ask for a high school graduation date under guidelines against age discrimination, one can ask for proof of graduation from college if that is a prerequisite for all candidates in the pool. Usually when people do not divulge a graduation date, they are masking a gap between graduation and their first job.

It is possible that Knight is just as good a candidate as O'Day—just a much worse resume writer! In any case, a take-home lesson here is that the resume is only a starting point. Certainly O'Day looks stronger, but an interview would reinforce O'Day's qualities, definitely remove Knight as a contender, or, possibly, show Knight as the better person for the job.

PHILIP R. O'DAY
1828 Lake Avenue
Columbus, OH 32812   (513) 848–1492   Phillybob@earthlink.net

Objective
A dynamic, creative, highly successful technical sales and marketing executive with seven years experience in operations, P&L, sales management, and personal selling looking for appropriate mid-management opportunity with a well-established company with ambitious goals and the corporate confidence to achieve them.

Operations VP, ZTech, Inc., August 1997 to present, San Jose, CA, and Columbus, OH

Responsibilities
- $27.3M in sales for hardware, software, and service contracts
- Managed domestic and international sales teams
- Supervised a sales team of technical sales engineers and support personnel
- Prepared and executed business, sales, marketing, and product development plans for entire company
- Managed budget of $2.6M

Accomplishments
- Increased sales 602 percent from $3.9M (1997) to $27.3M (2001)
- Integrated international sales and marketing operations into domestic operations, saving redundant costs of $650,000
- New software sales at 32 percent over base of $5.6M.
- Created and sold service contracts from $0 base to $1.6M
- Promoted from Sales Manager to Operations VP in January 2000

Senior Sales Engineer, June 1994 to July 1997 Kryptonix, Inc., Thousand Oaks, CA

Responsibilities
- Sold leading vector convergence product to aerospace industrial customers
- Acquired patents from Cal Tech and Jet Propulsion Laboratory
- Managed national accounts, including Boeing and Lockheed
- Developed pro forma P&L spreadsheets, analyzed current product for profitability
- Performed due diligence on product Kryptonix was considering acquiring

Accomplishments
- Acquired patents with projected revenue in excess of $53M (1995/97)
- Awarded "SE of the Year" with cash $50,000 and trip to Bali
- Created and launched customer database tracking program

Education
B.S. *cum laude* (Iowa State University) Electrical Engineering 1993, minor in Speech Communications
M.S. with honors (Stanford University) Computational Science, 1995

William Q. Knight
1828 Lake Avenue
Columbus, OH 32812   848–1492   BillyQ@earthlink.net

Operations VP, ZTech, Inc., 1997 to present San Jose, CA, and Columbus, OH

Responsibilities
- Over $27M in sales for hardware, software, and service contracts
- Managed domestic and international sales teams
- Conducted weekly staff meetings
- Traveled 100 percent as needed
- Liaison for international and domestic CEOs
- Served as co-chair of minority recruitment committee
- Supervised various teams of engineers and support personnel
- Prepared and executed business, sales, marketing, and product development plans for entire company
- Managed budget of approximately $3M

Accomplishments
- Substantially increased sales
- Saved substantial money with integration of domestic and international services
- Increased software sales to nearly $6M

Senior Sales Engineer, 1995-1996, Kryptonix, Inc., Thousand Oaks, CA

Responsibilities
- Sold leading vector convergence product to aerospace industrial customers
- Acquired patents from leading research centers
- Led the Seismographic Interpreter team
- Managed national accounts
- Traveled ten-state region
- Attended trade shows
- Ran field tests on Boron Substrate Analyzer
- Filed DOE and EPA reports
- Developed spreadsheets, analyzed current product performance
- Performed due diligence on product Kryptonix was considering acquiring

Education
B.S. *cum laude* Iowa State University
M.S. Stanford University

Sample Reference Check Sheet

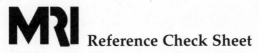 Reference Check Sheet

Candidate's   Date:
Name:

Name of   Telephone #:
Company:

Person   Title:
Contacted:

_____, this is _____ and I'm a search consultant with MRI Consultants. _____ has asked us to assist him/her in finding a new career opportunity. It is our policy to check references for all people who register with us, and I'd like to verify some of the information that he/she has given me. Let me assure you that _____ has signed a consent statement, allowing us to check his/her references and/or credit.

1. He/she lists his/her dates of employment with you from: Mo. _____ Yr. _____ to Mo. _____ Yr. _____. Is that correct?   ☐ Yes   ☐ No

2. What were his/her primary responsibilities? According to my information, he/she was also involved in [describe]. Would you say that accurately summarizes his/her responsibilities?   ☐ Yes   ☐ No
Comments:

3. _____ said his/her starting salary was $ _____ and that when he/she left, he/she was earning $ _____. Is that correct?   ☐ Yes   ☐ No
Comments (salary, bonuses, commissions):

4. How would you compare his/her results with others in similar functions? Were they:
☐ Excellent   ☐ Average   ☐ Below Average   ☐ Poor

5. Would you consider him/her to be:
☐ An industrious, hard worker   ☐ A person who did just enough to get by   ☐ A below average worker

6. Would you say his/her interpersonal relations with others on the job were:

    ☐ Excellent   ☐ Average   ☐ Below Average   ☐ Poor

7. (When applicable) How many people did he/she supervise directly? _____ Indirectly? _____

    Would you say he/she was a ☐ good supervisor? ☐ poor supervisor?

8. (When applicable) What responsibilities did _____ have in management decisions and policy formation?

9. _____ said he/she left your organization because [give reason]. Does that agree with your recollection of the matter?   ☐ Yes   ☐ No

10. Would you say that his/her attendance on the job was

    ☐ Excellent   ☐ Average   ☐ Below Average   ☐ Poor

11. What would you say are _____'s strong points or assets?

12. What area or areas did you see him/her improve while working there?

13. If you had an opening, would you re-employ_____?
    ☐ Yes ☐ No   If not, why not?

14. Is there anything else you'd like to tell me that might help in forming an accurate description of _____'s background and experience?

Thank the person for the information given and ask, "Do you have any critical staffing needs right now?" Or "Do you know of anyone who is interested in a career move?" Tell the person about MRI and how you work as a search consultant.

Summary: ☐ Good references ☐ Some reservations
☐ Definitely open to question

Comments:

FURTHER READING ON RECRUITING AND HIRING

Chapter 1: Before You Start Hiring, Have a Plan

Adams Streetwise Hiring Top Performers: 600 Ready-to-Ask Interview Questions and Everything Else You Need to Hire Right by Bob Adams and Peter Veruki (Adams Media Corporation, 1997).

The Agile Manager's Guide to Hiring Excellence (The Agile Manager Series) by Hardy Caldwell and John Hook (Velocity Publications, 1998).

Don't Hire Anyone Without Me! A Revolutionary Approach to Interviewing & Hiring the Best by Carol Quinn (Career Press, 2001).

The Fast Forward MBA in Hiring: Finding and Keeping the Best People by Max Messmer (John Wiley & Sons, 1998).

Finding, Hiring, and Keeping Peak Performers: Every Manager's Guide by Harry Chambers (Perseus Books, 2001).

Hire with Your Head: Using POWER Hiring to Build Great Teams (2nd ed.), by Lou Adler (John Wiley & Sons, 2002).

Hiring Excellence: Six Steps to Making Good People Decisions by Pat MacMillan (Navpress, 1992).

The Hiring Handbook by William Quirk (Panel Publications, 1994).

Hiring Right: A Practical Guide by Susan Herman (Sage Publications, 1994).

Hiring Smart: Beyond Just Hiring—Here Are Creative Ways to Build Your Team by Thomas Winninger (Prima Publishing, 1996).

Hiring Winners: Profile, Interview, Evaluate: A Three-Step Formula for Success by Richard Pinsker (The Saratoga Flier, Inc., 2001).

Impact Hiring by Frederick Ball and Barbara Ball (Prentice Hall, 2000).

Smart Hiring for Small Companies by Robert Wendover (Kendall/Hunt, 1988).

Topgrading: How Leading Companies Win by Hiring, Coaching and Keeping the Best People by Bradford Smart (Prentice Hall, 1999).

101 Hiring Mistakes Employers Make . . . and How to Avoid Them by Richard Fein (Impact Publications, 2000).

Chapter 2: Paint a Picture of the Perfect Hire

Critical Path Hiring: How to Employ Top-Flight Managers by Philip Matheny (Lexington Books, 1986).

45 Effective Ways for Hiring Smart! How to Predict Winners and Losers in the Incredibly Expensive People-Reading Game by Pierre Mornell and Regain Dunnick (Ten Speed Press, 1998).

Hiring Excellence: Six Steps to Making Good People Decisions by Pat MacMillan (Navpress, 1992).

Hiring Great People by Kevin Klinvex, Matthew Connell, and Christopher Klinvex (McGraw-Hill, 1998).

Hiring the Best by Ann McGill (McGraw-Hill, 1993).

Hiring Winners: Profile, Interview, Evaluate: A Three-Step Formula for Success by Richard Pinsker (The Saratoga Flier, Inc., 2001).

A Small Business Guide to Employee Selection: Finding, Interviewing, and Hiring the Right People (Self-Counsel Series) by Lin Grensing-Pophal (Self Counsel Press, 1991).

Chapter 3: Write a Motivating Ad

Recruiting for Success: Hiring and Keeping the Right Management Talent by American Productivity & Quality Center (American Productivity & Quality Center, 1998).

Smart Hiring: The Complete Guide to Finding and Hiring the Best Employees by Robert Wendover (Sourcebooks, 1998).

Chapter 4: Read, but Don't Rely on, Resumes

The Costs of Bad Hiring Decisions & How to Avoid Them by Carol Hacker (CRC Press—St. Lucie Press, 1998).

Hiring: More Than a Gut Feeling (Build Your Business Series) by Richard Deems (Career Press, 1995).

Hiring Smart: How to Conduct Background Checks (HR Executive Special Reports) by Philip Dickinson (M. Lee Smith Publishers LLC, 1997).

Pre-Employment Inquiries: Avoiding Pitfalls in the Hiring Process by Janet Little Horton and Victoria Corcoran (Education Law Association, 1985).

Chapter 5: Always Create a Pool of Candidates

The Difficult Hire by Dennis Doverspike and Rhonda Tuel (Impact Publications, 2000).

The Fast Forward MBA in Hiring: Finding and Keeping the Best People by Max Messmer (John Wiley & Sons, 1998).

A Small Business Guide to Employee Selection: Finding, Interviewing, and Hiring the Right People (Self-Counsel Series) by Lin Grensing-Pophal (Self Counsel Press, 1991).

Chapter 6: Use Recruiters to Raise the Quality of the Hiring Process

Now Hiring: An Employer's Guide to Recruiting in a Tight Labor Market (A BNA Special Report) by Linda Fernandez (Ed.) (Bureau of National Affairs Plus, 1989).

Recruiting for Success: Hiring and Keeping the Right Management Talent by American Productivity & Quality Center (American Productivity & Quality Center, 1998).

Chapter 7: Differentiate Talent and Ability from Skill and Experience

Build a Better Staff: Hiring, Evaluating and Firing Staff Members by Darla Struck and Jeff Stratton (Eds.) (Aspen Publishers, Inc., 1998).

Hiring: More Than a Gut Feeling (Build Your Business series) by Richard Deems (Career Press, 1995).

Hiring the Right Person for the Right Job by Cecilia Dobrish, Rick Wolf, and
Brian Zevnick (Franklin Watts, Incorporated, 1984).

*Hiring Top Performers—350 Great Interview Questions for People Who Need
People* by Carol Hacker (Carol A. Hacker & Associates, 1997).

*How to Hire the Right Person: A Practical and Step-by-Step Approach to the
Crucial Hiring Process* by Bonnie Russell (Simon & Schuster Australia,
1999).

101 Hiring Mistakes Employers Make . . . and How to Avoid Them by Richard
Fein (Impact Publications, 2000).

Chapter 8: Interview on Behavior and Experiences, Not on Hypotheses

*Adams Streetwise Hiring Top Performers: 600 Ready-to-Ask Interview
Questions and Everything Else You Need to Hire Right* by Bob Adams
and Peter Veruki (Adams Media Corporation, 1997).

High Impact Hiring: How to Interview and Select Outstanding Employees by
Del Still (Management Development Systems LLC, 2001).

Hiring the Best: A Manager's Guide to Effective Interviewing by Martin John
Yate (Adams Media Corporation, 1988).

*Hiring Top Performers—350 Great Interview Questions for People Who Need
People* by Carol Hacker (Carol A. Hacker & Associates, 1997).

Hiring Winners: Profile, Interview, Evaluate: A Three-Step Formula for Success
by Richard Pinsker (The Saratoga Flier, Inc., 2001).

Interviewing and Selecting High Performers: A Practical Guide to Effective Hiring
(Management Skills Series) by Larry Smalley (Jossey-Bass, 1997).

*The Manager's Book of Questions: 751 Great Interview Questions for Hiring the
Best Person* by John Kador (McGraw-Hill, 1997).

*Picking Winners: A Total Hiring System for Spotting Exceptional Performers
and Getting Them on Board* (Pathways, 3) by Steven Kneeland (How to
Books Ltd., 2000).

The Small Business Guide to Hiring Good People: Selection Interviewing by
Barbara Schoenberger and Lynn Baber (Eds.) (Schoenberger &
Associates, 1987).

The Smart Interviewer by Bradford Smart (John Wiley & Sons, 1990).

Successful Hiring: A Practical Guide to Interviewing & Selecting Employees by
Inland Management Services (Inland Management Services, 1997).

Chapter 9: Conduct a Structured Interview

Hiring the Best: A Manager's Guide to Effective Interviewing by Martin John Yate (Adams Media Corporation, 1988).

The Small Business Guide to Hiring Good People: Selection Interviewing by Barbara Schoenberger and Lynn Baber (Eds.) (Schoenberger & Associates, 1987).

The Smart Interviewer by Bradford Smart (John Wiley & Sons, 1990).

Successful Hiring Through Skillful Interviewing Techniques (workbook and three audiocassettes) by Susan Schroeer (Asher Gallant Pr, 1988).

The Ultimate How-to Guide: Interviewing & Hiring the Best Sales Professionals by Charles Rippin (Charles Rippin, 1999).

Chapter 10: Follow Legal and Ethical Guidelines in Hiring

The Americans with Disabilities Act: Hiring, Accommodating and Supervising Employees with Disabilities (Legal Issues for Business Series) by Mary Dickson and Kay Keppler (Eds.) (Crisp Publications, 1995).

The Complete Reference Checking Handbook: Smart, Fast, Legal Ways to Check Out Job Applicants by Edward Andler (AMACOM, 1998).

Complying with the ADA: A Small Business Guide to Hiring and Employing the Disabled (Wiley Small Business Editions) by Jeffrey Allen (John Wiley & Sons, 1993).

Diversity-Based Hiring: An Introduction from Legal, Ethical and Psychological Perspectives by C.M. Singer (Avebury, 1993).

Fair, Square & Legal: Safe Hiring, Managing, & Firing Practices to Keep You & Your Company Out of Court by Donald Weiss (AMACOM, 1999).

Hiring and Firing Book: A Complete Legal Guide for Employers by Steven Mitchell Sack (Legal Strategies Publications, 1993).

Pre-Employment Inquiries: Avoiding Pitfalls in the Hiring Process by Janet Little Horton and Victoria Corcoran (Education Law Association, 1985).

Chapter 11: Sell the Company to the Candidate

Competing for Employees: Proven Marketing Strategies for Hiring and Keeping Exceptional People by Kathleen Groll Connolly and Paul Connolly (Macmillan, 1992).

The Difficult Hire by Dennis Doverspike and Rhonda Tuel (Impact Publications, 2000).

How to Compete in the War for Talent: A Guide to Hiring the Best by Carol Hacker (InSync Press, 2001).

Now Hiring: An Employer's Guide to Recruiting in a Tight Labor Market (A BNA Special Report) by Linda Fernandez (Ed.) (Bureau of National Affairs Plus, 1989).

Picking Winners: A Total Hiring System for Spotting Exceptional Performers and Getting Them on Board (Pathways, 3) by Steven Kneeland (How to Books Ltd., 2000).

Topgrading: How Leading Companies Win by Hiring, Coaching and Keeping the Best People by Bradford Smart (Prentice Hall, 1999).

The War for Talent by Ed Michaels, Helen Handfield-Jones, and Beth Axelrod (Harvard Business School Press, 2001).

Chapter 13: Increase Your Knowledge of the Candidate Through Tests, Trials, Role Plays, and Projects

The Costs of Bad Hiring Decisions & How to Avoid Them by Carol A. Hacker (CRC Press—St. Lucie Press, 1998).

Hiring: More Than a Gut Feeling (Build Your Business Series) by Richard Deems (Career Press, 1995).

Pre-Employment Inquiries: Avoiding Pitfalls in the Hiring Process by Janet Little Horton and Victoria Corcoran (Education Law Association, 1985).

Successful Hiring: A Practical Guide to Interviewing & Selecting Employees by Inland Management Services (Inland Management Services, 1997).

Chapter 14: Always Check References

The Complete Reference Checking Handbook: Smart, Fast, Legal Ways to Check Out Job Applicants by Edward Andler (AMACOM, 1998).

The Costs of Bad Hiring Decisions & How to Avoid Them by Carol A. Hacker (CRC Press—St. Lucie Press, 1998).

Hiring Smart: How to Conduct Background Checks (HR Executive Special Reports) by Philip D. Dickinson (M. Lee Smith Publishers, 1997).

Pre-Employment Inquiries: Avoiding Pitfalls in the Hiring Process by Janet Little Horton and Victoria Corcoran (Education Law Association, 1985).

Chapter 15: Share Decisions on Hiring

People Investment: How to Make Your Hiring Decisions Pay Off for Everyone (PSI Successful Business Library) by Anita E. Worthington and E.R. Worthington (PSI Research—Oasis Press, 1992).

Chapter 16: Act with a Sense of Urgency

Picking Winners: A Total Hiring System for Spotting Exceptional Performers and Getting Them on Board (Pathways, 3) by Steven Kneeland (How to Books Ltd., 2000).

Chapter 17: Negotiate Terms and Make an Offer

A Field Guide on the Hiring Process from Both Sides of the Desk by Jim L. Dalton (Uniquely Yours, 2000).

INDEX

A

Ads/advertising: Internet, 4, 13–14; paid/discounted by recruiters, 31; placing, 4; requirements of effective, 14–16; writing motivating, 13–17

Ads/advertising characteristics: calling potential applicants to action, 14–15; including Equal Employment Opportunity statement, 16; lead with highest competitive approved salary range, 15; listing key accountabilities, 15–16; listing key job requirements, 15; requiring cover letter and resume, 16; specifically forbids phone calls, 16

Applicants: ads which call for action, 14–15; equal treatment of each, 56; making travel arrangements for, 5; phone screening, 4–5; refusing phone calls from, 16; reviewing resume/applications of, 4; setting up first round interviews of, 5. *See also* Candidates

Application review time, 4

Avoiding hiring defects: be wary of halo effect, 8; beware of tendency to mirror, 7–8; consider candidate's values and company values/ culture, 10–11; do list background behavioral attributes of model candidate, 8–9; separate behavior attributes/trained skills of ideal candidate, 9–10; think about diverse people in organization, 10

ABOUT THE AUTHOR

WALTER ANTHONY DINTEMAN graduated from West Virginia University with a degree in education, concentrating in history and English. After teaching junior high school English and social studies, he sold college textbooks for Scott, Foresman & Company in all or parts of six states. At Scott, Foresman he was promoted to acquisitions editor and then executive editor for social science. In 1980 he was "Editor of the Year." Mr. Dinteman returned to the South and to the field as a sales supervisor for Harper & Row before joining Addison-Wesley as southern regional manager, a post he held for eleven years, during which he won numerous sales awards and promotion to divisional vice president in 1993. In 1995 he joined John Wiley & Sons, where he was both southeast district manager and national college recruiter. In 2000, he formed Management Recruiters International/Sales

Consultants of Asheville, Inc., a full-service recruiting firm serving the print publishing and new media fields. With over twenty-five years' experience as an editorial and sales manager and, lately, as a full-time recruiter, Mr. Dinteman has accumulated deep knowledge of the recruiting and hiring process that he has distilled as *Zero Defect Hiring*.